Yorkshire Terrier
and Australian Silky Terrier

A guide to selection, care, nutrition,
rearing, training, health, breeding,
sports and play

A must for both owners and people who are
interested in finding a suitable dog breed.

© 2007 About Pets bv
P.O. Box 26, 9989 ZG Warffum, the Netherlands
www.aboutpets.info
E-mail: management@aboutpets.info

ISBN: 9789058218100

First edition 2007

Photos: About Pets photography team

Acknowledgements:
Photos: Jolanda van Lierop, Isabelle Francais, Silvia van de Meer, Hanna Koevoets, Roel and Magda, Henny van de Berg, Fred and Corita Rombouts, Kingdom Books and Veen-Buijks Fam.
Anatomic illustrations: Hill's
Graphs: Courtesy of Royal Canin

Contents

Foreword

The book you are holding is a basic owners' manual for everyone owning a
Yorkshire or an Australian Silky terrier and also for those who are considering
buying a Yorkshire or an Australian Silky terrier. What we have done in this
book is to give the basic information to help the future owner of a Yorkshire or
an Australian Silky terrier look after his or her pet responsibly.
Too many people still buy a pet before really understanding what they're about
to get into.

This book goes into the broad history of the Yorkshire and the Australian Silky
terrier, their breed standards and some pros and cons of buying a Yorkshire or
an Australian Silky terrier. You will also find essential information on feeding,
initial training and an introduction to reproduction. Finally we give attention to
day-to-day care, health and some breed-specific ailments.

Based on this information, you can buy a Yorkshire or an Australian Silky
terrier, having thought it through carefully, and keep it as a pet in a responsible
manner. A properly brought-up and well-trained dog is more than just a dog.
Invest a little extra in a puppy training course or an obedience course. There
are also excellent books available that go deeper into certain aspects than is
possible here.

About Pets

In general

The Yorkshire terrier is a small, longhaired toy dog, which is also called Yorkie by its fans. Its character is lively, intelligent, sometimes overconfident and very friendly. It is also alert when it feels that something is wrong.

The Australian Silky terrier has been developed from the Yorkshire terrier, which is why it is also dealt with in this book.

Origin of the Yorkshire terrier

About 125 years ago, this appealing terrier entered the scene in Yorkshire, Great Britain. The breed is a creation of the working men from Leeds and Halifax. People worked in agriculture until the Industrial Revolution changed family life in 1750. People were on the move looking for work, e.g. in coal mines or textile factories and they brought their dogs with them. Among others, these were the Clydesdale terrier and Paisley terrier, which are believed to be ancestors of the Yorkshire terrier.

No records were kept about breeding programs. It seems fairly certain that the Sky terrier, the old English Terrier and the Scottish terrier are all part of the Yorkie's lineage. The Maltese, Cairn terrier, the Black and Tan Toy terrier or Manchester terriers and the now extinct Waterside terrier are also mentioned. The exact origins are uncertain. The breeding methods were probably the best kept family secrets: the more unique, the better the price.

In the past, these terriers were a little bigger and heavier and were used for pest control, especially against rats. They were also used for hunting small mammals.

In the very beginning of their show career, the Yorkies were referred to as Scotch terriers. In 1874, the first dogs were registered as an individual breed under this name in the British Kennel Club stud book. In 1886, the name *Yorkshire terrier* was finally established.

A dog called Huddersfield Ben (named after the town of Huddersfield), bred by Mr Eastwood, and was a show winner and rat catcher. Because of his show reputation, he became a well known stud. Together with his owner Mr M.A. Foster, he managed to get lots of attention at shows. Ben was born in 1865 and after a happy life lasting 6 years, he died in 1871. Ben is regarded as the progenitor of the breed. The breed was officially registered as early as 1886.

This little dog with its glamorous coat became a popular dog during Victoria's reign over the British Empire (1837 - 1901). In these days the dog's weight was approximately 9 kilo (20 lb). Around 1840, competitions in rat pits were popular. During this time, the weight of the dog was reduced to 4.5 kilo (10 lb). Ratting expeditions were another popular pastime.

The dogs were first bred for uniformity, and later on they were bred smaller and smaller. The weight is now only 1 to 2.5 kilos.

Besides these show-dwarfs, there are, of course, still some bigger individuals.

In 1889, the first Yorkie with the title *American Champion* was Bradford Harry. It's no surprise to learn that he was a great-great-grandson of Huddersfield Ben. This dog, imported from England, was owned by P.H. Coombs of Bangor, Maine.

In 1898, the first Yorkshire Terrier Breed Association was formed. In 1932, three-hundred Yorkies were already registered. In 1957, this had already increased to 2,313 dogs. The year 1970 marked a break-through in the development of the breed, as the Yorkshire terrier was the most popular breed of this year.

Rat catchers

When thinking about rats, some people automatically think of the plague or Black Death. The plague is caused by a bacterium: Yersinia pestis. It usually infects rodents, which means that the fleas settling on these animals also become infected. Rodents such as rats, mice and rabbits die quickly when infected. In need of *tasty* blood the fleas find new sources in humans when too few rodents are available.

In Europe, the plague returned regularly from 1347 – 1722. In the second half of the 17th century, an arsenic ratbane helped destroy suspect rodent populations. Fortunately the Yorkie was not a rat catcher during periods of the plague. People had become aware of the danger that rats and their fleas brought along. Cats had become scarce during times of witchcraft. The plague seemed to be gone, but the rat flourished.
The long hair of the Yorkie comes in very handy. Rats will try to defend themselves and the long hair protects the dog against a biting rat. The rat had great difficulties defending itself with just a mouth full of dog hair. That's why these longhaired dogs were quite useful in those days.

Origin of the Australian Silky terrier

The Australian Silky terrier originates in Australia. The Australian Silky terrier was developed from the Yorkshire terrier, which was imported around the turn of the century, and the Australian terrier. The Australian terrier is said to be a melting pot of several British dog breeds, for example the Cairn terrier and the Dandie Dinmont. Other dogs - the so called *Broken Haired terrier* - were used as pest control on Australian sheep farms. It is fairly safe to assume that the *Broken Haired terrier* is the basis of the Australian terrier.

The Australian terrier was a popular dog at the beginning of the 20th century. In 1908, the breed was presented at a show in Melbourne, but it was not before 1933 that it was awarded champion status.

Crossbreeding the Australian terrier with the Yorkshire terrier created the Australian Silky terrier. The main goal was to improve the blue-and-tan colour. When looking at the coat quality, it is quite likely that the Clydesdale terrier had some influence. This lively, elegant, loyal, affectionate, energetic and intelligent dog has a coat of fine, silky texture, which parts on the back.

The breed got its present name in 1955. Due to its perfect adaptation to city life, the dog had previously been given the name Sydney Silky terrier. In 1907, the breed was presented at an Australian dog show. Two years later, in 1909, the first breed standard was written. It took until 1959 to get the breed recognised in the USA. The breed combines the best characteristics of both the Australian terrier and the Yorkshire terrier. These active, inquisitive terriers have a more luxurious coat than the Yorkies. They are lightly built, compact dogs, which have fairly short legs. They can have both upright and hanging ears, but only the dogs with upright ears appear at dog shows.

The UK Kennel Club and their Breed Standards

What does the UK Kennel Club do?
To say it in their own words: "The Kennel Club is committed to developing and supporting a nation of responsible dog owners. As well as

organising events and campaigns to help dog owners meet their responsibilities, the Kennel Club also produces a range of literature to assist the dog-owning public."

What is the use of a breed standard?

The Kennel Club answers: "The basis of breed shows is the judging of dogs against the Breed Standard, which is the prescribed blueprint of the particular breed of dog. For all licensed breed shows, the Kennel Club Breed Standards must be used for the judging of dogs."

More about the UK Kennel Club breed standards: "The Breed Standards are owned by The Kennel Club, and all changes are subject to approval by The Kennel Club General Committee. New Breed Standards, for newly recognised breeds, are drawn up once the breed has become sufficiently established within the UK. Careful research is conducted into the historical background, health and temperament of any new breed before Kennel Club recognition is granted. The Kennel Club currently recognises 196 breeds. Upon recognition, breeds are placed on the Imported Breed Register until they are deemed eligible for transferral to the Breed Register".

A standard provides a guideline for breeders and judges. It is something of an ideal that dogs of each breed must strive to match. With some breeds, dogs are already being bred that match the ideal. Other breeds have a long way to go. There is a list of defects for each breed. These can be serious defects that disqualify the dog, in which case it will be excluded from breeding. Permitted defects are not serious, but do cost points in a show.

The UK Kennel Club Breed Standard for the Yorkshire Terrier

General Appearance
Long-coated, coat hanging quite straight and evenly down each side, a parting extending from nose to end of tail. Very compact and neat, carriage very upright conveying an important air. General outline conveying impression of vigorous and well proportioned body.

Characteristics
Alert, intelligent toy terrier.

Temperament
Spirited with even disposition.

Head and Skull
Rather small and flat, not too prominent or round in skull, nor too long in muzzle; black nose.

Eyes
Medium, dark, sparkling, with sharp intelligent expression and placed to look directly forward. Not prominent. Edge of eyelids dark.

Ears
Small, V-shaped, carried erect, not too far apart, covered with short hair, colour very deep, rich tan.

Mouth
Perfect, regular and complete scissor bite, i.e. upper teeth closely overlapping lower teeth and set square to the jaws. Teeth well placed with even jaws.

Neck
Good reach.

Forequarters
Well laid shoulders, legs straight, well covered with hair of rich golden tan a few shades lighter at ends than at roots, not extending higher on forelegs than elbow.

Body
Compact with moderate spring of rib, good loin. Level back.

Hindquarters
Legs quite straight when viewed from behind, moderate turn of stifle. Well covered with hair of rich golden tan a few shades lighter at ends than at roots, not extending higher on hind legs than stifles.

Tail
Customarily docked
Docked: Medium length with plenty of hair, darker blue in colour than rest of body, especially at end of tail. Carried a little higher than level of back.
Undocked: Plenty of hair, darker blue in colour than rest of body, especially at end of tail. Carried a little higher than level of back. As straight as possible. Length to give a well balanced appearance.

Gait/Movement
Free with drive; straight action front and behind, retaining level top line.

Coat
Hair on body moderately long, perfectly straight (not wavy), glossy; fine silky texture, not woolly. Fall on head long, rich golden tan, deeper in colour at sides

of head, about ear roots and on muzzle where it should be very long. Tan on head not to extend on to neck, nor must any sooty or dark hair intermingle with any of tan.

Colour
Dark steel blue (not silver blue), extending from occiput to root of tail, never mingled with fawn, bronze or dark hairs. Hair on chest rich, bright tan. All tan hair darker at the roots than in middle, shading to still lighter at tips.

Size
Weight up to 3.2 kgs (7 lbs).

Faults
Any departure from the foregoing points should be considered a fault and the seriousness with which the fault should be regarded should be in exact proportion to its degree and its effect upon the health and welfare of the dog.

Note
Male animals should have two apparently normal testicles fully descended into the scrotum.

July 2001

Breed standard by courtesy of The Kennel Club of Great Britain

The UK Kennel Club (interim) Breed Standard of the Australian Silky Terrier

General Appearance
Compact, moderately low-set, medium length with refined structure; sufficient substance to suggest ability to hunt and kill domestic rodents. Straight silky hair parted from nape of neck to root of tail, presenting a well-groomed appearance.

Characteristics
Terrier-like, keen, alert, active.
Temperament. Very friendly, quick and responsive.

Head and Skull
Moderate length, slightly shorter in length from tip of nose to between eyes than from there to top rear of occiput. Moderately broad between ears; skull flat, without fullness between eyes. Nose black.

Eyes
Small, round, as dark as possible, not prominent, keen intelligent expression.

Ears
Small V-shaped, with fine leathers, high on skull and pricked; entirely free from long hair.

Mouth
Jaws strong, with a perfect, regular and complete scissor bite, i.e. upper teeth closely overlapping lower teeth and set square to the jaws. Teeth even and not cramped, lips tight and clean.

Neck
Medium length, refined, slightly arched. Well covered with long silky hair.

Forequarters
Shoulders fine, well laid back, well angulated upper arms fitting snugly to ribs; elbows turn neither in nor out; forelegs straight with refined round bone, set well under body with no weakness in pasterns.

Body
Slightly longer than height. Level top line; well sprung ribs extending back to strong loins. Chest of moderate depth and breadth.

Hindquarters
Thighs well developed. Stifles well turned; when viewed from behind, the hocks well let down and parallel.

Feet

Small, well padded and cat-like. Closely knit toes with black or very dark toenails.

Tail

Customarily docked.
Docked: Carried erect; not over-gay. Free from long feathering.
Undocked: Carried erect, not over-gay. Free from long feathering. Length to give an overall well-balanced appearance.

Gait/Movement

Free, straight forward without slackness at shoulders or elbows. No turning sideways of feet or pasterns. Hindquarters have strong propelling power with ample flexibility at stifles and hocks. Viewed from behind, movement neither too close nor too wide.

Coat

Straight, fine and glossy; silky texture; length of coat 13 - 15 cms (5 - 6 ins) from behind ears to set-on of tail desirable. Legs, from knees and hocks to feet, free of long hair. Fine silky top-knot, not falling over eyes. Long fall of hair on foreface and cheeks undesirable.

Colour

Blue and tan, grey-blue and tan, the richer these colours the better. Blue on tail very dark. Distribution of blue and tan as follows:
Silver-blue or fawn top-knot, tan around base of ears, muzzle and on side of cheeks; blue from base of skull to tip of tail, running down forelegs to near knees and down thighs to hocks; tan line showing down stifles, and tan from knees and hocks to toes and around vent. Blue colour must be established by 18 months of age.

Size

Most desirable weight about 4 kgs (8 - 10 lbs). Height approximately 23 cms (9 ins) at withers, bitches may be slightly less.

Faults

Any departure from the foregoing points should be considered a fault and the seriousness with which the fault should be regarded should be in exact proportion to its degree and its effect upon the health and welfare of the dog.

Note

Male animals should have two apparently normal testicles fully descended into the scrotum.

July 2001

Breed standard by courtesy of The Kennel Club of Great Britain.

Purchase

Once you've made that properly considered decision to buy a dog, there are several options. Should it be a puppy, an adult dog, or even an older dog? Should it be a bitch or a male dog, a pedigree dog or a cross?

Are you looking for a companion or a real show dog? Of course, the question also comes up as to where to buy your dog. Are you going to buy it from a private person, a reliable breeder, or would you maybe even get it from an animal asylum? It is important for you and the animal that you sort out these things in advance. You want to find a dog that fits in with your situation. With a puppy, you choose a playful, energetic housemate, which will adapt easily to its new surroundings. If you want something a little quieter, an older dog is a good choice.

Pros and cons

The long silky coat of these two breeds needs plenty of care every day. This can be both an advantage and a disadvantage. Some people do not enjoy spending a lot of time grooming their dog, whereas others particularly enjoy making their dog as beautiful as possible. A well cared for Yorkie or Silky will get everybody's attention.

Neither the Yorkie nor the Silky has an undercoat. That means that they do not have a moulting period, but they need to be trimmed once in a while. The lack of an undercoat also has the advantage that these dogs don't spread that wet-dog-smell when they got wet. A disadvantage is that these dogs have problems keeping themselves warm and that they will need some extra protection (jacket) when it gets cold.

These dogs are very small and they fit into any house. This is, of course, an advantage. They don't need very much exercise, but it is better for them if they build up a good condition. They also both have a true terrier character and thus need a consequent, honest upbringing. Both breeds are very focused on their master and love to be with him as much as possible. They will follow you around all day long. Both breeds become very old and fifteen years is no exception. Both visitors and the postman are announced with loud barking.

Male or female?

Whether you choose a male or a female puppy, or an adult dog or bitch, is an entirely personal decision. A male typically needs more leadership because he tends to be more dominant by nature. He will try to play boss over other dogs and, if he gets the chance, over people too. In the wild, the most dominant dog or wolf is always the leader of the pack. In many cases this is a male. A bitch is much more focussed on her master, as she sees him as the pack leader.

A puppy test is good for defining what kind of character a young dog will develop. During a test one usually sees that a dog is more dominant than a bitch.
You can often quickly recognise the bossy, the adventurous and the cautious characters. So visit the litter a couple of times early on. Try to pick a puppy

that suits your own personality. A dominant dog, for instance, needs a strong hand. It will often try to see how far it can go. You must regularly make it clear who's the boss, and that it must obey all the members of the family. If you want to visit shows with your new companion, then you should choose an adventurous type and not the most timid puppy from the nest.

When bitches are sexually mature, they will go into season. On average, a bitch is in season twice a year for about two or three weeks. This is the fertile period when she can become pregnant. Particularly in the second half of her season, she will want to go looking for a dog to mate with. A male dog will show more masculine traits once he is sexually mature. He will make sure other dogs know what territory is his by urinating as often as possible in as many places as he can. He will also be difficult to confine if there's a bitch in season nearby. However, as far as normal care is concerned, there is little difference between a dog and a bitch.

Puppy or adult?
After you've made the decision for a male or a female, the next question arises. Should it be a puppy or an adult dog? Your household circumstances usually play a major role here.

Of course, it's great having a sweet little puppy in the house, but bringing up a young dog costs a lot of time. In the first year of its life it learns more than during the rest of its life. This is the period when the foundations are laid for elementary matters, such as house-training, obedience and social behaviour. You should reckon on, especially in the first few months, having to devote a lot of time to caring for your puppy, and bringing it up. You won't need so much time with a grown dog. It has already been brought up, but this doesn't mean it doesn't need correcting from time to time.

A puppy will no doubt leave a trail of destruction in its wake for the first few months. With a little luck, this will only cost you a number of rolls of wallpaper, some good shoes and a few socks. In the worst case you'll be left with some chewed furniture. Some puppies even manage to tear curtains from their rails. With good upbringing this "vandalism" will quickly disappear, but you won't have to worry about this if you get an older dog.

The greatest advantage of a puppy, of course, is that you can bring it up your own way. And the upbringing a dog gets or doesn't get is a major influence on its whole character. Finally, financial aspects may play a role in your decision. A puppy is generally much more expensive than an adult dog, not only in purchase price but also in maintenance. A puppy needs to go to the veterinarian more often for the necessary vaccinations and check-ups.

Overall, bringing up a puppy costs a good deal of energy, time and money, but you have its upbringing in your own hands. An adult dog costs less money and time, but its character has already been formed. You should also try to find out about the background of an adult dog. Its previous owner may have formed its character in somewhat less positive ways.

Two dogs?

Having two or more dogs in the house is not just nice for us, but also for the animals themselves. Dogs get a lot of pleasure from each others' company. After all, they are pack animals.

If you're sure that you want two young dogs, it's best not to buy them at the same time. Bringing a dog up and establishing the bond between dog and master takes time, and you need to give a lot of attention to your dog in this phase. Having two puppies in the house means you have to divide your attention between them. Apart from that, there's a danger that they will focus on one another rather than on their master. Buy the second pup when the first is almost an adult.

Two adult dogs can easily be brought into the home at the same time, as long as they are used to each other. If this in not the case, then they need to get used to each other first. It is best to let the dogs get acquainted with each other on neutral territory. You will thus not encounter the problem that one of them will try to guard the territory. On neutral ground, e.g. a friend's garden where neither dog has been before, both dogs will be basically equal. You can then take them home and let them sort out the hierarchy among themselves.

Do not interfere in any quarrels, however. This might be a human reaction, but for the dog that is higher in the hierarchy it is as if its position is threatened. It will only show more dominant behaviour, with all the nasty consequences this might have. Once the hierarchy has been sorted, most dogs will get along very well.

Getting a puppy when the first dog is somewhat older often has a positive effect on the older dog. The influence of the puppy almost seems to give it a second childhood. The older dog, if it's been well brought up, can help with the upbringing of the puppy. Dogs like to imitate each other's behaviour. Don't forget to give both dogs the same amount of attention. Take the puppy out alone at least once per day during the first eighteen months. Make sure the older dog has enough opportunity to get some peace and quiet. It won't always be able to keep up with the speed of such an enthusiastic youngster. A puppy also needs to have the breaks put on once in a while.

The combination of a male and a female needs special attention. It is best to take two dogs of the same sex, as this will prevent a lot of problems. Neutering and spaying is, of course, an option, but it is a final one. You will never be able to breed with a neutered or spayed animal. Neutering and spaying also have a big influence on the hormone balance, which can even change the coat structure in a way that it will get tangled or matted more easily. Get all the information you need before taking such a step.

A dog and children
Dogs and children are a great combination. They can play together and get great pleasure from each other. Moreover children need to learn how to handle

living beings; they develop respect and a sense of responsibility by caring for a dog or another pet.

However sweet a dog is, children must understand that it is an animal and not a toy. These small terriers are quite fragile. A dog isn't comfortable when it's being messed around with. So make it clear what a dog likes and what it doesn't. Look for ways the child can play with the dog, perhaps a game of hide-and-seek where the child hides and the dog has to find it. Even a simple tennis ball can give enormous pleasure. Children must learn to leave a dog in peace when it doesn't want to play any more. A Yorkie or Silky must also have its own place where it's not disturbed. Have children help with your dog's care as much as possible. A strong bond will be the result.

The arrival of a baby also means changes in the life of a dog. Before the birth you can help get the dog acquainted with the new situation. Let it sniff at the new things in the house and it will quickly accept them. When the baby has arrived, involve the dog as much as possible in day-by-day events, but make sure it gets plenty of attention too.

Never leave a dog alone with young children! Crawling infants sometimes make unexpected movements, which can easily frighten a dog. And infants are hugely curious, and may try to find out whether the tail is really fastened to the dog, or whether its eyes come out, just like they do with their cuddly toys. Yorkies and Silkies always remain dogs: they will defend themselves when they feel threatened.

A dog and cats

Despite the fact that their body language is very different, dogs and cats can actually get on a lot better with each other than many people think. For example, a dog lying on its back is submissive. A cat lying on its back is not at all submissive, but makes sure that it has its best weapons of defence, i.e. its claws, at its disposal. However, dogs and cats have one thing in common: they growl when they are angry, and both animals understand this.

As far as nutrients are concerned, dogs and cats must not share each other's food. Dog food may lack high enough levels of taurine, which is essential for cats. Dogs and cats must also not share a food bowl, as a dog will not tolerate another animal sharing its bowl. A persistent kitten might therefore get a serious ticking off from your dog. Playing together is fine, but you must prevent your pets eating together.

Some dogs will love to chase your cat around. You must prohibit this behaviour from the very beginning. The cat also has its rights and the dog will have to learn not to chase everything that moves. You can take your dog to special classes to help you deal with this.

Some dogs, this is not a characteristic of any particular breed, love to eat cat faeces (coprophagia). To prevent your dog eating from the cat litter, place the litter box in another room, where only your cat has access. Or place the litter box between two pieces of furniture in a manner that prevents your dog gaining access

Where to buy your dog

There are various ways of acquiring a dog. The decision for a puppy or an adult dog will also define for the most part where you buy your dog.

If it's to be a puppy, then you need to find a breeder with a litter. If you choose a popular breed, such as the Yorkie or Silky, there is choice enough. But you may also face the problem that there are so many puppies on sale that have only been bred for profit's sake. You can see how many puppies are for sale by looking in the regional newspaper every Saturday. Some of these dogs have pedigrees, but many don't. Breeders often don't watch out for breed-specific illnesses and in-breeding; puppies are separated from their mother as fast as possible and are thus insufficiently socialised. Never buy a puppy that is too young, or whose mother you weren't able to see.

Fortunately there are also enough bonafide breeders of Yorkshire terriers and Australian Silky terriers. Try to visit a number of breeders before you actually buy your puppy. Ask if the breeder is prepared to help you after you've bought your puppy, and to help you find solutions for any problems that may come up.

Finally, you must realise that a pedigree is nothing more or less than a proof of descent. The Kennel Club also issues pedigrees to the young of parents that suffer from congenital conditions, or that have never been checked for these. A pedigree says nothing about the health of the parent dogs.

What to watch out for

Buying a puppy is no simple matter. You must pay attention to the following:

- Never buy a puppy on impulse, even if it is love at first sight. A dog is a living being that will need a lot of care and attention over a long period, for more than ten years. It is not a toy that you can put away when you're done with it.
- Take a good look at the mother. Is she calm, nervous, aggressive, well cared-for or neglected? The behaviour and condition of the mother is not only a sign of the quality of the breeder, but also of the puppy you're about to buy.
- Avoid buying a puppy whose mother was kept only in a kennel. A young dog needs as many stimuli and experiences as possible during its early months, including family life. It can thus get used to humans, other pets and different sights and sounds. Kennel dogs miss these experiences and have not been sufficiently socialised.
- Always ask to see the parents' papers (vaccination certificates, pedigrees, official health examination certificates).
- Let the breeder know if you have show ambitions with your future dog.
- Never buy a puppy younger than eight weeks.
- Put all agreements with the breeder in writing. A model agreement is available from the breed association.

Shopping list
- Collar
- Lead
- ID tag
- Blanket
- Water bowl
- Food bowl
- Poop scoop
- Dry food
- Canned food
- Comb
- Brush
- Toys
- Dog basket
- Indoor kennel

Travelling

There are a few things to think about before travelling with your dog. While one dog may enjoy travelling, another may hate it. While you might enjoy going on holidays to far-away places, it is questionable whether your dog does, too.

That very first trip

The first trip of a puppy's life is also the most nerve-wrecking. This is the trip from the breeder's to its new home. If possible, pick up your puppy in the morning. It then has the whole day to get used to the new environment. Ask the breeder not to feed the puppy that day. The young animal will be overwhelmed by all kinds of new experiences. Firstly, it's away from its mother; it's in a small room (the car) with all its different smells, noises and strange people. So there's a big chance that the puppy will be carsick this first time, with the annoying consequence that it will remember travelling in the car as an unpleasant experience.

So it's important to make this first trip as pleasant as possible. When picking up your puppy, always take someone with you who can sit in the back seat with the puppy on his or her lap and talk to it calmly. If it's too warm for the puppy, a place on the floor at the feet of your companion is ideal. The pup will lie there relatively quietly and may even take a nap. Ask the breeder for a cloth or something else from its nest, which carries a familiar scent. The puppy can lie on this in the car, and it will also help if it feels lonely during the first nights at home.

If the trip home is a long one, then stop for a break once in a while. Let your puppy roam and sniff around on the lead, have a little drink and, if necessary, let it do its business. Do take care to lay an old towel in the car. It can happen that the puppy, in its nervousness, may urinate or be sick.

It's also good advice to give a puppy positive experiences with car journeys as soon as possible. Make short trips to nice places where you can walk and play with it. It can be a real nuisance if your dog doesn't like travelling in a car. You will always come across situations when your dog needs to travel in the car, such as when taking it to the veterinarian or to visit friends.

Taking your dog on holiday

When making holiday plans, you also need to think about what you're going to do with your dog during that time. Are you taking it with you, putting it into a boarding kennel or leaving it with friends? In any event there are a number of things you need to do in good time.

If you want to take your dog with you, you need to be sure in advance that it will be welcome at your holiday home, and also check what rules there are. If you're going abroad it will need certain vaccinations and a health certificate, which normally need to be done four weeks before departure. You must also be sure that you've made all the arrangements necessary to bring your dog back home to the UK, without it needing to go into quarantine under the rabies regulations. Your vet can give you the most recent information. If your trip is to southern Europe, ask for a treatment against ticks (you can read more about this in the *Parasites* chapter).

Although dog owners usually enjoy taking their dog on holiday, you must seriously ask yourself whether the dog feels that way too. Yorkies and Silkies certainly don't always feel comfortable in a hot country. Days spent travelling in a car are also often not their preference, and some dogs suffer badly from carsickness. There are good medicines for this, but it's questionable whether you're doing your dog a favour with them.

If you do decide to take it with you, make regular stops at safe places during your journey, so that your dog can have a good run. Take plenty of fresh drinking water with you, as well as enough of the food your dog is used to. Never leave your dog in the car when the sun is shining. The temperature can climb fast and this can very quickly be an awful and life-threatening situation for your dog. If you can't avoid it, park the car in the shade as far as possible and leave a window open for a little fresh air. Even if you've taken these precautions, frequently check on your dog and never stay away longer than is strictly necessary.

If you're travelling by plane or ship, make sure in good time that your dog can travel with you and what rules you need to observe. You will need some time to make all the arrangements.

Maybe you decide not to take your dog with you, and you then need to find somewhere for it to stay. Arrangements for a place in a boarding kennel need to be made well in advance. There will be certain vaccinations required, which need to be given a minimum of one month before the stay. If your dog can't be accommodated in the homes of relatives or friends, it might be possible to have an acquaintance stay in your house. This also needs to be arranged well in advance, as it may be difficult to find someone who can do this. Always ensure that your dog can be traced should it run away or get lost while on holiday. A little tube with your address or a tag with home and holiday address and a mobile telephone number can prevent a lot of problems.

Moving home

Dogs generally become more attached to humans than to the house they live in. Moving home is usually not a problem for them. But it can be useful to let the dog get to know its new home and the area around it before moving.

If you can, leave your dog with relatives, friends, or in a boarding kennel on the day of the move. The chance of it running away or getting lost is then practically non-existent. Once you have completed your move, you can pick your dog up and let it quietly get familiar with its new home and environment. Give it its own place in the house at once and it will quickly adapt. During the first week or so, always walk your dog on a lead, because an animal can get lost in new surroundings too. Always take a different route so it quickly gets to know the neighbourhood.

Don't forget to get your new address and phone number engraved on your dog's tag. Send a change of address notice to the institution that has the microchip.

Feeding

A dog will actually eat a lot more than just meat. In the wild it would eat its prey complete with skin and fur, including the bones, stomach, and the intestines with their semi-digested vegetable material. In this way the dog supplements its meat menu with the vitamins and minerals it needs. This is also the basis for feeding a domestic dog.

Basic principles of dog food

In general

Dogs have always been primarily carnivores (meat eaters). A minor part of their daily diet consists of vegetable material or the vegetable-based content of their prey's stomach and intestines. In the past, dogs kept as pets used to be fed the remains of the family dinner.

Nowadays, most dogs are fed a diet of dry food and canned food. The diets of our domestic dogs and cats have changed remarkably over the last fifteen years. There has been a clear increase in expertise and the foodstuffs have become increasingly differentiated. To fully understand the effects of foods, it is important to have some understanding of the anatomy and physiology of dogs.

Anatomy and physiology of the dog's digestive tract

Ingested food first passes into the mouth, where it is crunched. Dogs have no lateral movement in their jaws and therefore cannot chew, but during this crunching, the food is divided into smaller bits and moistened with saliva. The dog's saliva does not contain digestive enzymes, so true digestion does not yet start in the mouth.

After swallowing, the food passes through the oesophagus to the stomach, where it is mixed and kneaded with gastric acid, i.e. one of the digestive juices. The gastric acid breaks down the proteins present in the food and kills off a large number of potentially harmful micro-organisms present in the food.

Once the food pulp has been kneaded through thoroughly and fulfils a number of chemical requirements, the closing muscle (pylorus) of the stomach relaxes and the food passes through into the duodenum.
The duodenum is the first part of the small intestine. Here important digestive juices such as gall and the pancreatic juices are added to the food pulp. The gall juices help with the digestion of fat and the pancreatic juices contain enzymes which help with the digestion of carbohydrates, proteins and fat.
Enzymes are substances which are produced by the animal itself and which help with chemical transformation during digestion.

The small intestine must furthermore be differentiated into the jejunum, ileum and caecum (appendix). The wall of the small intestine contains cells which provide the digestive juices. The wall has plenty of folds to provide as large a surface area as possible, where bacteria, which help in the digestive processes, and enzymes find a place to attach to.
The actual digestion occurs in the small intestine and the foodstuffs are cut down into tiny pieces which can be absorbed.

After being absorbed by the cells in the intestines, the nutrients are passed on to the blood, which transports the nutrients to the liver. The liver functions as a sort of traffic agent, which decides what needs to happen to the different nutrients and then sends them to the right place.

The large intestine (colon) follows on from the small intestine. The most important function here is to absorb the water from the food pulp. The intestine ends in the closing muscle (anus) via the rectum.

Food
Food contains many nutrients which can be divided into six important groups: proteins, fats, carbohydrates, minerals, vitamins and water. Life cannot exist without water. Water does not actually contain any extra

nutrients, unless it is mineral water, which can be very rich in certain minerals.

Proteins

Proteins look like a pearl necklace, consisting of different amino acids (the pearls). The amount and type of amino acids determines the characteristics of the protein in question.
The presence of nitrogen in all amino acids is important for the development of tissue.

Proteins fulfil many functions in the body; they are the most important components of tissue, hormones and enzymes. Furthermore, they fulfil other important roles by maintaining water levels in the body, removing toxins and maintaining a good defence system.
Proteins are found in both vegetable (grains, legumes, yeast) and animal (meat, fish, poultry, eggs) form. An adult dog must have at least 20g protein/1000kcal food (8% protein) in the dry matter of its food (NRC 2006) to keep up the maintenance level.
In fact, if you want to ensure optimum health, maximum performance and a beautiful appearance, this percentage must be somewhat higher.

The story that protein is bad for dogs has long been proven a myth. This was based on research in rats, but at the end of the 70s, research showed that the kidney metabolism of dogs is by no means as sensitive as that of rats. Since 1993, we have also known that proteins do not have a detrimental influence on growth.

On the contrary, proteins, together with the right exercise, contribute to healthy muscles, which in turn stabilise the skeleton. This is a very important consideration for such conditions as hip dysplasia, for example.
Plenty of proteins therefore contribute to your dog's health.
A shortage of proteins will lead to anaemia, low resistance to illness, loss of muscle tissue, etc.

A shortage of proteins is caused not only by insufficient absorption, but also through increased breaking-down of proteins, which may be caused by many forms of stress (mental or physical strain on the individual animal).
An influence of protein on behaviour is not yet clear.

Fat

The most important function of fats is to provide energy. Besides this, fats also provide unsaturated fatty acids. Fatty acids fulfil important functions in the nervous systems and the skin's metabolism, among other things. Fats in the food are very easily digested by dogs; in general they digest as much as 95 - 98%. Dogs, just as humans, prefer food with a higher fat content, which is why it is often added to dog food to make it tastier. Fat is also important as it stores some vitamins.

Carbohydrates

Carbohydrates always originate in vegetable material.
Starch and sugar are well-known examples of carbohydrates.
You can differentiate between digestible carbohydrates (starch, simple sugars) and non-digestible carbohydrates (cellulose, pectin), which come from the cell membranes and fibres of plants. Carbohydrates improve the transport of the food pulp in the intestines by stimulating the membrane of the intestines. This stimulates the peristaltic movement of the intestines.
A disadvantage is that they increase the volume of the faeces, as they also hold a lot of water. A good compromise are the fibres which function as such throughout the major part of the intestines, and are then broken down at the last stage by bacteria in the large intestine. The fibres are broken down into substances which partly function as a source of food for the cells of the large intestine. Beet pulp, for example, contains these valuable fibres.

Minerals

Minerals only play a minor role in your dog's diet as far as the amount is concerned, but they are absolutely vital. Because minerals are needed in such small amounts, mistakes are easily made.
Minerals are divided into macro-minerals and micro-minerals or trace elements. Calcium (Ca) and phosphorus (P) are well-known macro-minerals. They fulfil an important role in building up the skeleton and, depending on the physiological phase, must be provided by the food in a fixed relation to each other. As phosphorus is of vegetable origin, it can often not be absorbed from the food, as in this form phosphorus cannot be absorbed by dogs (phytate).

Other important macro-elements include: magnesium (Mg) (skeleton, enzymes), sodium (Na), potassium (K) and chlorine (Cl). Some examples of micro-minerals include: iron (Fe) (blood, oxygen transport), copper (Cu) (creation of pigment, blood), zinc (Zn) (enzymes, skin), manganese (Mn) (enzymes), iodine (I) (thyroid hormone) and selenium (Se) (muscle tissue, antioxidant).

Vitamins

Vitamins can be of both vegetable and animal origins. Vitamins are divided into water-soluble and non-water-soluble vitamins. Vitamins are also required only in very small amounts and dogs can produce a number of vitamins themselves. Below, we will list a number of important vitamins and their functions.

Some important functions of vitamins

	function	shortage	excess
vitamin A	fertility, skin and eyes	fertility problems, night blindness	abnormal bone metabolism vitamin K deficiency
vitamin D3	bone metabolism	abnormal bone metabolism	abnormal bone metabolism, kidney malfunction
vitamin E	with Se protection, muscle cells, anti-oxidant	fertility problems, muscle dystrophy	
vitamin K	blood clotting	haemorrhages	
vitamin C	collagen metabolism, resistance, mucous membranes	connective tissue damage, haemorrhages, liver necrosis	
B1 (thimaine)	carbohydrate metabolism, nervous system	anorexia, circulation problems, diarrhoea, atrophic reproductive organs	
B2 (riboflavine)	catalyst, energy production, protein metabolism	anorexia, growth delays, circulation problems	
PP (niacine)	catalyst, resistance, skin and mucous membranes	skin problems, anorexia, diarrhoea	
B3 (pantothene acid)	part of coenzyme A, Krebs-cycle	alopecia, anorexia, diarrhoea	
B6 (pyridoxine)	catalyst protein metabolism	skin problems, haematological problems	
biotine	catalyst fatty acid synthesis	coat and skin problems	
folic acid	catalyst AZ synthesis	haematological and skin problems	
B12 (cyanocobalamine)	catalyst cystine/ methiomine metabolism	anaemia, alopecia, growth problems	

Energy

All organic processes require energy. This energy is needed for the body to function, produce tissue and to maintain body temperature, for example. The energy required must be provided by food. In principal, dogs eat until they have fulfilled their energy requirements. However, due to causes such as boredom, the feeding regime and tastiness of the food, there are many dogs that eat more than they need and become fat and heavy. It is therefore important to regularly check your dog's condition.

A dog will store energy reserves as fat on the ribcage. On short-haired dogs, you must be able to see the last two ribs, and on long-haired dogs you must be able to feel the ribs.

Start feeding your dog with the amount recommended on the food packaging, check your dog's condition once per week and adapt it as necessary. Increase the amount of food if you feel the ribs too clearly, and decrease the amount if you can no longer feel the ribs easily. Particularly puppies of breeds prone to skeletal growth problems must be somewhat on the thinner side while growing up.

Industrial food

Industrial dog foods can be divided into three categories depending on their moisture content: moist, semi-moist and dry food. Moist foods contain 70 - 85% water. Their high moisture content makes them very tasty for dogs, but they spoil more easily. The quality is more difficult to maintain than with dry food. The transport is also a disadvantage for the environment and for the owner: four times as much volume needs to be transported. This type of food is also relatively expensive.

Semi-moist food is dry enough that it doesn't have to be packed into cans. There are no real advantages to this type of food. Dogs might accept it somewhat more easily than dry food, but it does spoil quite easily due to its higher moisture content. Due to their increased moisture content, frozen foods may also be added to this category.

Dry foods are the most economical and are also not prone to turning mouldy, which means that they keep for a comparatively long time. The specific manufacturing process makes it easier to ensure constant high quality levels. Technically speaking, mixers belong to dry food until they have had water added. At this point, they also spoil quite quickly.

If you want to compare different types of food with each other, you will need to look at the dry matter (= product without water) contents and ingredients.

It is very difficult to judge the quality of dog food. The packaging does not provide all the information and may also not contain any quality claims. It is therefore a matter of trust and you might want to request some further information from the manufacturer. The amount of faeces also gives an indication: the more faeces, the lower the food quality.

This, however, does not apply to fibre-rich foods, such as diet foods, light foods, senior foods and diabetic foods.

Food quality

There are a number of important points as regards the quality of dog food: the digestibility, the biological value (degree to which the nutrients can be absorbed into the tissue), the manufacturing process and the circumstances under which the food is kept until consumption.

Different terminology is used to indicate quality levels. At the moment, the product range includes super premium, premium, products for the medium segment and products for the economical segment. The lower the quality, the lower the price per kilogram.

Top quality can only be delivered by manufacturers who have the best raw materials available, who conduct thorough research and who have a technologically advanced manufacturing process.

The first threat to the quality is oxidization of the ingredients. Light, oxygen and warmth are threats to food quality. Anti-oxidants therefore do a good job and the user must also ensure hygienic handling of the food.

Good-quality food is packaged in an airtight packaging, which also keeps out the light, it has a batch code and you can tell the best before and the manufacture dates.

Physiological phases

Good feeding must be adapted as well as possible to the physiological phase of the individual dog. After all, the physiological phase it is in determines what a dog needs.

A growing dog must produce a lot more tissue and therefore needs more building blocks than an adult dog.

All these growth processes require a lot of energy, which means that the energy need is also higher. Depending on the size of the dog, it will grow for 7 to 18 or even 24 months. During the growing period the puppy's digestive system is not fully developed and so can only cope with small volumes of food. It is therefore important that the food is both energy dense (which allows for a smaller feeding volume) and balanced in nutrients for that age and stage in development.

Puppies from a number of usually larger breeds have an increased risk of bone-related growth problems and must therefore be fed specifically adapted food. It is also important to keep these puppies slim when they are growing.

Reproduction and lactation are highly demanding on the bitch and, considering that she has to produce both offspring and milk, you can imagine that her energy needs increase a lot. From the 6th week of the pregnancy, you will therefore need to adapt the amount you feed.

Energy demands also increase if your dog is very active. If there is a lot of stress on muscle tissue, it will need to be repaired from time to time. There is also increasing wear on the blood, which means that more nutrients are

needed to produce plenty of blood cells. If you keep your dog in an outdoor kennel, it might also require more energy, as it will lose warmth more easily and it might be more active due to being kept outdoors.

By having a close look at the needs of dogs in different physiological phases, it is possible to develop a food which fulfils specific requirements under certain circumstances. Obviously, such dog food requires a lot more research and high-quality raw materials, which will be reflected in a somewhat higher price. Adequate dog food will ensure optimum health and resistance and is therefore always worth the asking price.

Besides the physiological phase, the size of the dog also matters. Pedigree dogs, of course, have set size standards and on mongrels the size depends on the parent animals. Research has shown that there are many differences between small and large dogs; both in terms of susceptibility to health problems and in anatomy and physiology. The manufacturers of the best dog foods take these differences into account. To give just a few examples of the physiological differences between large and small dog breeds:

	Small dog	Difference*	Large dog
Growth period	8 months	3	24 months
Range of growth	20x birth weight	5	100x birth weight
Length canine tooth	4-5 mm	3	15-16 mm
Energy needs	132 Kcal/kg BW**	3	45 Kcal/kg BW**
Weight digestive tract	7% BW**	>2	2.8% BW**
Life expectancy	> 12 years	+/- 3	7 years

* Difference = factor   ** BW = body weight

Of course, breeds have their specific size requirements, and every breed also has its own characteristics, such as a special coat or even breed-specific conditions. Breed-specific foods are therefore becoming increasingly popular. These foods are based on the special nutritional needs of the breed and some foods also contain substances which help to prevent breed-specific conditions developing.

Over the last few years, increasing attention has been paid to the possible preventative effect of dog food. Certain substances are added to the food, for example to increase the burning of fat (L-carnitine), to prevent diarrhoea in puppies (zeolite), to support the cartilage (glucosamine and chondroitine sulphate), etc.
The right food can therefore make a major contribution to your dog's health.

Important guidelines

In general
Buy food only in an undamaged package and have experts (vet, pet shop owner or breeder) advise you. Buying in bulk might be economical, but make sure that you have a food bin. Put a week's supply in a bucket, for example, and place the rest in a food bin in a dark, cool, place. Always make sure that you use up or throw away the last bit and clean out the bin regularly!

Puppy food
Buy the most suitable food for your puppy. The basis for a healthy adult life is laid in the growth period and food plays an important role here. Feed your puppy special puppy food at least as long as it is still growing in length (6 to 24 months, depending on the breed). If your puppy belongs to a breed which is sensitive to growth problems, feed it food which was specifically developed for puppies of that breed or size to keep the risk of problems developing as small as possible.

Adult dog
Choose the food which best suits your dog and adapt the amount you feed to its condition.

Pregnant dog

The food requirements of the bitch increase from the 6th week of pregnancy. In the past, bitches were often fed puppy food in the last stage of the pregnancy or during lactation. However, with today's range of puppy foods, they might not all be suitable, so get expert advice on how best to feed your pregnant bitch.

Older dog

The food requirements of older dogs change quite a lot. Scientifically speaking, older dogs need more easily digestible food, which stimulates the intestines, a normal protein content with high biological value and some support for the heart, the skeleton and to improve resistance to illness.

Puppies, pregnant bitch and mother

Amount of food during pregnancy and suckling period

To ensure that the weight increase is no more than 20% on large bitches and no more than 30% on small bitches, it is important to keep a close eye on the weight of your pregnant bitch.

The more the weight increases, the higher the risk of problems during the birth. During pregnancy and suckling, the bitch must be fed a correctly composed diet to ensure that her food reserves are not completely exhausted. If she is fed an incorrect diet, the bitch will have far more trouble recovering from this very demanding period.

During pregnancy

A bitch is pregnant for approximately 63 days. Her food needs start to increase at around the 5th or 6th week of pregnancy. About 25% of the foetus develops during the first 6 weeks of the pregnancy; the remaining 75% of the foetus develops from weeks 6 to 9.

During the last trimester, your bitch will have a particularly high need for:
Energy: + 50 to 70%
Proteins: + 170 to 180 %
Minerals: ++ (calcium, phosphorus)
Vitamins: ++

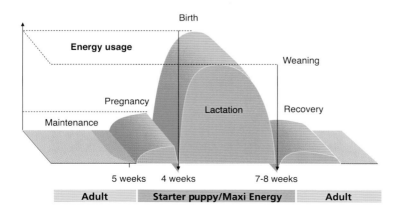

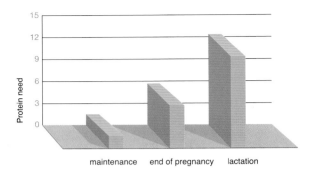

Protein need

maintenance   end of pregnancy   lactation

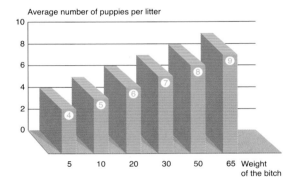

Average number of puppies per litter

5   10   20   30   50   65 Weight
                                     of the bitch

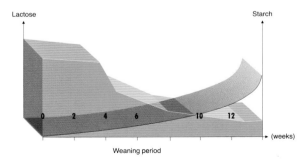

Lactose   Starch

Weaning period

(weeks)

During suckling

The suckling period lasts for 4 to 5 weeks, and the puppies gradually suckle less from the 4th week on. While suckling her offspring, the bitch will have a much higher energy need, as she must also produce the food for them. The mother's milk is very rich in energy and proteins. It is therefore important that the bitch is fed a diet which is high in energy and proteins, and which is very easily digestible. The actual food requirements vary a lot and primarily depend on the size of the litter. The food needs of a suckling bitch may be as follows:

Energy: + 325%
Proteins: + 725%
Minerals: ++++ (calcium, phosphorus)
Vitamins: ++++

To prevent digestive problems, it is advisable to feed the bitch the same food from the last part of the pregnancy until the time that the puppies are fully weaned. The bitch's intestines are particularly sensitive to food changes during this important period. Within 24 hours, a puppy suckles more than twenty times from its mother. The bitch must produce 20 to 25% of a puppy's weight in milk to feed one puppy for one day. So multiply this by the number of puppies in the litter.

The bitch may be fed ad lib during the suckling period, but do keep an eye on her condition.

Colostrum is the first milk that the bitch produces after the puppies are born. It is therefore very important that the puppies drink their mother's milk within the first 24 hours after birth. The colostrum contains anti-bodies against infections, which gives the puppies a good start to build up their own solid resistance. If the bitch produces too little milk, you will need to supplement it with special puppy milk.

Puppy during weaning

Right after being born, the puppies depend entirely on their mother's milk as their only food source to stay alive.

It is very important to check your puppies' growth during the first few days by weighing them at exactly the same time every day. Weaning must go very smoothly, so that the puppy and its organs get used to a completely new diet. When the puppy must change from a liquid diet to a solid diet, it is advisable to do this via an extra step.

Energy: + 50 to 70%
Proteins: + 170 to 180%
Minerals: ++ (calcium, phosphorus)
Vitamins: ++

The increasing nutritional needs are best fulfilled by feeding the bitch a specifically composed diet from the fifth or sixth week on. Besides more energy, the bitch also needs more proteins and she needs a concentrated and easily digestible diet, as the uterus pushes onto the stomach during pregnancy, which decreases the stomach volume. The bitch therefore can no longer deal with large amounts of food.

Weaning - an important period

The first step in weaning begins after the third week, when you can start feeding the puppies small amounts of moistened food. During the weaning period, the puppies are quite prone to diarrhoea, which is at least partly due to their limited ability to digest starch. Compared to an adult dog, they only have a 5 - 10% ability to digest starch (see picture). To minimise the risk of diarrhoea and to ensure optimum digestion, feed the puppy a food which is easily digestible and which has a low starch content.

Ready-made foods

It's not easy for a layman to put together a complete menu for a dog, including all the necessary proteins, fats, vitamins and minerals in just the right proportions and quantities. Meat alone is certainly not a complete meal for a dog, as it contains too little calcium. A continuous calcium deficiency will lead to bone defects, and for a fast-growing puppy this can lead to serious skeletal deformities. If you put its food together yourself, you can easily give your dog too much in terms of vitamins and minerals, which can also be bad for your dog's health.

You can avoid these problems by giving it ready-made food of a good brand. These products are well balanced and contain everything your dog needs. Supplements, such as vitamin preparations, are superfluous. The amount of food your dog needs depends on its weight and activity level. You can find guidelines on the packaging. Split the food into two meals per day if possible, and always ensure that there's a bowl of fresh drinking water next to its food.

Give your dog the time to digest its food and don't let it outside straight after a meal. A dog should never play on a full stomach. This can cause bloat (torsion

or gastric torsion): because of excessive gas content the stomach becomes overstretched.

Because the food needs of a dog depend, among other things, on its age and way of life, there are many different types of dog food available. There are light foods for less active dogs, energy foods for working dogs and senior foods for the older dog. There is also special food for smaller dog breeds such as the Yorkie and the Silky. The manufacturers have taken the size of a miniature dog's muzzle into consideration when designing these feeds. The bits are somewhat smaller and the food is concentrated, so that miniature breeds receive all the necessary nutrients. The smaller packaging also prevents the food turning bad.

Canned foods, mixers and dry foods

Ready-made foods available at pet shops or in the supermarket can roughly be split into canned food, mixer and dry food. Whichever form you choose, ensure that it's a complete food with all the necessary ingredients. You can see this on the packaging.

Most dogs love canned food. Although the better brands are composed well, they do have one disadvantage: they are soft. A dog fed only on canned food will not benefit from the gently abrasive effects of dry food and may potentially more quickly develop problems such as plaque, and/or periodontitis. Besides canned food, give your dog hard foods at certain times or a chew especially designed for the oral care of your dog.

Mixer is a food consisting of chunks, dried vegetables and grains. Almost all moisture has been extracted. The advantages of mixer are that it is light and keeps well. You add a certain amount of water and the meal is ready. A disadvantage is that it must definitely not be fed without water. Without the extra fluid, mixer will absorb the fluids present in the stomach, with serious results. Should your dog manage to get at the bag of mixer or dry chunks and enjoy its contents, give the dog small amounts of water - a half cup - over small time (20 - 30 minutes) intervals.

Dry chunks have also had the moisture extracted but not as much as mixer. The advantage of dry foods is that they are hard, forcing the dog to crunch, removing plaque and massaging the gums.

Dog chew products
Naturally, once in a while you want to spoil your dog with something extra. Don't give it pieces of cheese or sausage as these contain too much salt and fat. There are various products available that a dog will find delicious and which are also healthy, especially for its teeth. You'll find a large range of varying quality in the pet shop.

The butcher's left-overs
The bones of slaughtered animals have traditionally been given to the dog, and dogs are crazy about them, but they are not without risks. Pork and poultry bones are weak. They can splinter and cause serious injury to the intestines. Beef bones are more suitable, but they must first be cooked to kill off dangerous bacteria.
Pet shops carry a range of smoked, cooked and dried abattoir residue, such as pigs' ears, bull penis, tripe sticks, oxtails, gullet, dried muscle meat, and hoof chews. Due to its size, the butcher's leftovers are often not suitable for small dog breeds such as the Yorkshire terrier and the Silky terrier.

Fresh meat
If you do want to give your dog fresh meat occasionally, never give it raw, but always boiled or roasted. Raw or not fully cooked pork or chicken can contain life-threatening organisms. Chicken can be contaminated by the notorious salmonella bacteria, while pork can carry the Aujeszky virus. This disease is incurable and will quickly lead to your pet's death.

Cowhide and buffalo hide chews

Dog chews are usually made of cowhide or buffalo hide. The hide is knotted and pressed into chews. Your dog can enjoy a wide variety of chews, including shoes, twisted sticks, lollies and balls. They are nice to look at and a pleasant change. Make sure that the chews you buy are suitable for small dogs.

Munchie sticks

Munchie sticks are green, yellow, red or brown coloured sticks of varying thicknesses. They consist of ground buffalo hide with a number of often undefined additives. Dogs usually love them because these sticks have been dipped in the blood of slaughtered animals. The composition and quality of these between-meal treats is not always clear. Some are fine, but some have been found to contain high levels of cardboard and even paint residues. Choose a product whose ingredients are clearly labelled. The disadvantage of some of these sticks is that they can discolour the hair around the muzzle. They are thus less suitable for show dogs.

Overweight?

Recent investigations have shown that many dogs are overweight. A dog usually becomes too fat because of over-feeding and lack of exercise. Medicines or disease are rarely the cause. Dogs that become too fat are often given too much food or too many treats between meals. Gluttony or boredom can also be a cause, and a dog often puts on weight following neutering of spaying. Due to changes in hormone levels it becomes less active and consumes less energy. Finally, simply too little exercise alone can lead to a dog becoming overweight.

You can use the following rule of thumb to check whether your dog is overweight: you should be able to feel its ribs, but not see them. If you can't feel its ribs then your dog is much too fat. Overweight dogs live a passive life, they play too little and tire quickly. They also suffer from all kinds of medical problems (problems with joints and the heart for example). They usually die younger too. So it's important to make sure your dog doesn't get too fat. Always follow the guidelines on food packaging. Adapt them if your dog is less active or gets lots of snacks. Try to make sure your dog gets plenty of exercise by playing and running with it as much as you can. If your dog starts to show signs of putting on weight, you can switch to a low-calorie food. If it's really too fat and reducing its food quantity doesn't help, then a special diet is the only solution.

Care

Good daily care is very important for your Yorkie or Silky. A well cared-for dog is far less at risk of becoming ill. Looking after your dog is not just a necessity, but also a pleasure: master and dog give each other all their attention. It is also a great moment for a game or a cuddle.

The coat

Yorkshire puppies are born with a short coat. The longer hairs develop slowly. The steel-blue colour is still black on puppies, but they already display the tan markings. At the age of approximately three to six months, the colour changes from black to steel-blue, but it can happen as late as at twelve to eighteen months. At the age of two to three years, the coat has its final colour. The colour change starts on the head, which lightens up to a slate-blue and finally gets its final colour. If your puppies are the right colour too early, they will probably become too light over time. Silky terriers are born completely black and with smooth hair.

Taking care of your dog's coat includes daily brushing or combing and checking for parasites (fleas). How often your dog needs to be brushed or combed depends on the length of the coat. You keep your Yorkie or Silky only as a companion and don't have much time for intensive grooming? Have your dog's coat clipped at a grooming parlour. It is better to have a dog with a clipped coat (although this is not really appropriate for the breed) than to have one with a tangled and matted coat.

A perfectly groomed coat is the Yorkie's and Silky's most striking feature and the most important characteristic of these breeds. A layman might assume the ribbon on the dog's head is for decoration only. There is, however, more to it to maintain the coat correctly. Use the right equipment for your grooming sessions.

Grooming your dog

Bathing

Before actually making the dog wet you must be sure the coat is properly combed: small objects can cause matting. A pup has to get used to water. Introduce your pup to the water in a playful manner and it will even start to enjoy the bathing sessions. Provide your dog with a bath mat even if you put it in the kitchen sink. The dog will stand more securely on this. Another important issue is taking good care no shampoo will run into your dog's eyes. Ask your pet shop for advice in finding a no-tear dog shampoo with a correct pH balance, preferably on mink-oil base. Do not use any other shampoo but dog shampoo. Wet your dog thoroughly, and then apply the shampoo. Wash the belly, the private parts and feet. The rest of the body comes last. Make sure you don't mess up the coat. Rinsing is very important. Soap residue may cause coat and skin problems. Rinse until you no longer see any cloudy water coming of.

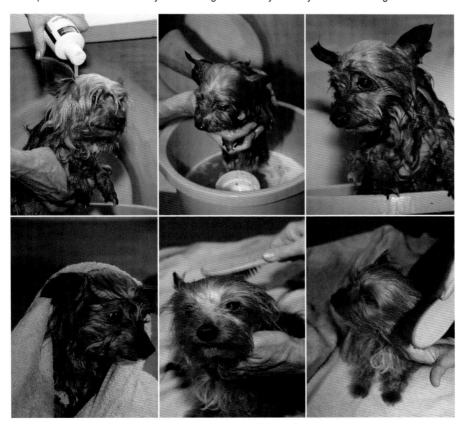

Now you can apply a conditioner. Be patient and follow the instructions on the bottle regarding waiting time, then rinse thoroughly. Some dogs will shake on command. It's easy to teach your pup when walking in (summer) rain. Each time the dog wants to shake itself, you say "shake!".

Gently squeeze your hands down the body and most water will drip away. First pat the dog with a towel. Then wrap a warm towel around the body, so the dog will not get cold. Make sure the washing and drying area are comfortably warm.

Blow-drying the coat layer by layer will do the job. Be careful not to point the blow dryer in the eyes. Start with the head and the back. Then turn the dog on its side and dry the belly and legs. Set the hairdryer on the lowest setting and make plenty of circular movements, as the warm air can quickly become too hot. To give your dog a fine appearance and, most of all, to keep the hair out of the eyes, put the bow on top of your dog's head. Only let your dog outside when it is completely dry, as dogs can catch colds too!

Up to this point, the guideline applies equally to pet and show dogs.

Paper curlers

A show dog needs lots more attention because the long hair must be kept clean and is not supposed to break.

When the dog is still small, you can start with daily brushing. Get the dog used to laying on its back. You handle the coat from bottom layer to top layer.

When your pup is seven months old, you can put some coat oil into the coat. Buy special coat oil. Put a little on a brush and gently brush it into the coat. A little oil will do, too much oil makes the dog feel cold.

Before going to a show, you wash the oil out of the coat.

In order to keep the coat clean and prevent the hair from breaking, wrap the hair into paper curlers. This special paper is available in the grooming parlour or in a good pet shop. Fold a sheet of the silky paper, measuring 25 by 25 cm. Lay a lock of hair in each strip of paper, and fold the right and the left side of the paper over the hair. When rolled up, each package is held together with a rubber band. You need to repeat this routine every day. If you don't, matting and painful tangles will develop. After unrolling, you need to brush the coat.

Take care: You are not supposed to leave your puppy or adult dog unattended on a table, sofa or other higher-levelled place. It can easily fall or try to jump off and get hurt.

Your vet can prescribe special medicinal shampoos for some skin conditions. Always follow the instructions. To prevent skin and coat problems, it is important to fight fleas well. Don't just treat the fleas on your dog, but also in its environment (see the chapter *Parasites*). Coat problems can also be a result of an allergic reaction to certain feed ingredients. If this is the case, your vet will prescribe a hypoallergenic diet.

Teeth

A dog needs to be able to eat properly to stay in good condition. It thus needs healthy teeth. Regularly check your dog's teeth and molars. If you think that all is not well, contact your vet immediately. Regular feeds of hard dry food will help to keep your dog's teeth clean and healthy. You can buy special dog chews, which prevent the development of tartar and ensure a fresh breath.

The most effective way to care for your dog's teeth is to brush them. You can use a special dog toothbrush for this, but some gauze wrapped around your finger will also do the trick. If you get your dog used to having its teeth cleaned at an early age it will get used to it quite quickly. You can also get an older dog used to having its teeth cleaned. With a dog chew as a reward it certainly won't mind.

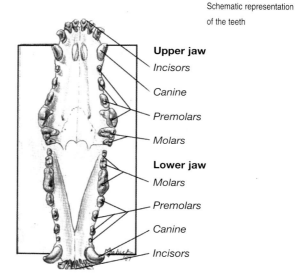

Schematic representation of the teeth

Upper jaw
Incisors

Canine

Premolars

Molars

Lower jaw
Molars

Premolars

Canine

Incisors

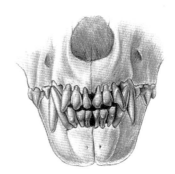

Left: profile of the teeth
Right: front view of the teeth

Nails

If your dog walks on hard ground a lot, its nails will normally wear down by themselves. If this is not the case, then you need to cut its nails. It will certainly not do any harm to check the length of the nails on a regular basis, especially if your dog doesn't go out on the streets a lot. If you can push a paper between the ground and your dog's nail when it is standing, then it is the right length.

Nails that are too long can hinder your dog. It can injure itself when scratching. They therefore need to be cut. You can do this with special nail scissors from the pet shop. Be very careful not to cut the nail off too far, as you can easily cut into the quick, in which case it will bleed profusely. It is quite difficult to see where the quick begins in the nails of Yorkies and Silkies, because their nails have a dark colour. If you are unsure about cutting your dog's nails, let the vet or grooming parlour do it.

Eyes

You need to clean your dog's eyes every day. Sleepies and bits of dried tear fluid can gather in the corners of the eye. You can easily remove these by wiping downwards with your thumb. If you don't like doing this, use a bit of tissue paper.

Keeping your dog's eyes clean only takes a few seconds a day, so don't miss it! If the sleepies are yellow and slimy, then your dog probably has a serious irritation or infection. You can usually solve this problem quite easily with eye drops, which you can get at your veterinarian. Prevent irritations by keeping the eyes clear of hair. You can do this by tying your dog's hair together with a bow on its head.

Ears

When looking after their dogs, many people forget the ears. They need to be checked at least once a week, though. If they are very dirty or contain a lot of wax, you will need to clean them. Do this preferably with a clean cotton cloth moistened with some warm water or baby oil. Don't use cotton wool, because of the fluff it leaves behind. Never enter the ear canal with an object!

If the hair in the ears causes problems, it is best to remove it. Carefully pull it out between your thumb and index finger. If you neglect looking after your dog's ears, there's the risk of an ear infection. A dog that scratches its ears a lot might be suffering from dirty ears, an ear infection or ear mites. You will need to take it to the veterinarian as soon as possible.

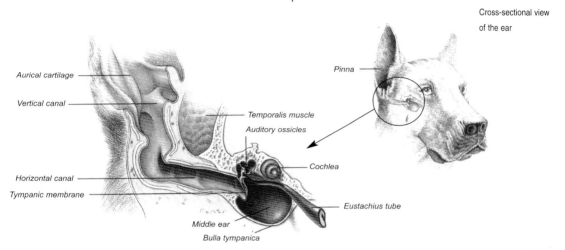

Cross-sectional view of the ear

Aurical cartilage

Vertical canal

Pinna

Temporalis muscle

Auditory ossicles

Cochlea

Horizontal canal

Tympanic membrane

Eustachius tube

Middle ear

Bulla tympanica

Grooming equipment:
- small pin brush (stainless steel)
- small rubber backed slicker brush
- natural bristle brush
- 1 big and 1 small stainless steel comb
- scissors with rounded tip
- toenail clipper
- coat conditioner
- silky curler paper
- rubber bands
- portable hair dryer
- ribbons
- bows

Rearing

It is very important that your dog is well brought up and obedient. This not only makes it more fun for you to be with your dog, but it also makes it more pleasant for other people.

A puppy can learn in a playful manner what it must and must not do. Praise and consistency are two very important tools when bringing up a dog. When you reward your puppy for good behaviour with your voice, a pat or something tasty, it will soon learn to be obedient. A puppy course can be very helpful here. When dealing with your dog, it is also useful to know something about the life of dogs, i.e. wolves, in the wild.

In the wild, wolves, the ancestors of our dogs, live in packs. They are therefore used to living in a group. Our domestic dogs view their families as their packs. In fact, our dogs see us as dogs, too. Every pack has a hierarchy. This means that there is one boss, the alpha animal, and all the other animals are ranked according to importance, right to the lowest position, the omega animal. There is a constant battle for the alpha spot in the pack. When you take a dog into your home, it is therefore very important to make it clear where its place is in the family. This is simply done by following twelve rules. In this chapter, we deal with the rules of the pack, what they are, how you can apply them and what you can do and what you better not do.

The rules of the pack

Rule 1
The Alpha dog sleeps where it wants and no-one is to approach it
An animal high up in the hierarchy can choose its own place to rest. This place is always respected by the animals lower in the hierarchy. If an inferior animal comes close to a superior animal which is resting, the latter will growl to make it clear that the inferior animal must not approach.
If the inferior animal approaches anyway, there is real risk that the superior animal will bite. This rule not only applies to resting and sleeping. The superior animal always has access to places which are prohibited to the inferior animal. The alpha animal is therefore not always the official pack leader; it is the animal highest in hierarchy present at that moment.

Advice:
• Never let your dog sleep in your bed
• The bedroom should actually be entirely forbidden territory for your dog.
• You can also prohibit access to other parts of the house. This makes it clear to the dog that you are higher in the hierarchy.
• If your dog lies on a chair which you want to sit on, simply sit down without saying anything. If necessary, sit on your dog.

Don't
• Never try to take away your dog's safe place.
• Never let your dog take away your place.
• Never let your dog refuse people access to certain places.

Rule 2
The alpha male has the highest position.
In a pack of dogs, you can often see that the pack leader lies somewhat higher than the rest of the pack, as if he wants to have a good overview over the pack. The alpha male thus demonstrates his high position. Domestic dogs also often want to lie on a somewhat higher place and they might try to climb onto the headrest of your sofa in an attempt to demonstrate that they have a high position. Dogs which are lower down in the hierarchy would never dare to demonstrate such behaviour. Dogs demonstrate what position they hold within the pack not just by lying on a higher place, but also with their general attitude.

Advice

- When you notice that your dog wants to lie on a higher position while you are present, do not allow it.
- If, for example, you are sitting on the stairs and your dog comes to sit with you, make sure that it does not sit on a higher step than you.

Don't

- Never let your dog crawl onto your lap without permission.
- Never pick up your dog to a higher position in the presence of another dog or human, as this will give your dog an artificial and undeserved higher position.

Rule 3

The alpha male eats first. The others get the left-overs, unless the alpha decides to keep everything for himself.

When the pack has caught a large prey, it is not necessarily divided up democratically. The alpha animal always eats first, possibly together with the alpha bitch at most. The rest of the pack must wait until the leader has finished.

The alpha male will decide when the rest of the pack gets its food. He might also decide that the others don't get anything at all. In this case, he simply puts the remains of the prey somewhere else and moves away. In fact, the alpha animal challenges the inferior animals to take the food. If an inferior animal dares to approach the food, the alpha animal will growl loudly and bite the inferior animal in the neck to correct it, or grab the food away from it to display his higher position.

Advice

- Prepare your dog's food and place it out of reach. Then you go and have dinner first.
- Only feed your dog when the whole family has finished. Preferably, first give the *stay* command and then allow your dog to approach its food.
- Place toys on the floor close to your dog.

When it wants to take the toy, you grab it away. Repeat this a few times. Your dog will soon stop trying to take the toy. This is the moment when your dog acknowledges your superiority.

Don't
- Never feed your dog anything while the family is having dinner. This gives the dog the same position in the hierarchy as the members of the family.
- Be careful with food envy! Never take food away from your dog and stay away from its food bowl when it is eating.

Food envy
Many dogs refuse to give up things they carry in their mouth (food, toys). If you do try to take these things from your dog, it will growl. We can often see the same behaviour in dogs that are eating. When you approach your dog's bowl, it will growl. This behaviour is called food envy.

Rule 4
Playing, not fighting, is the way to establish hierarchy.
A dog can determine and confirm hierarchical positions during play. For young dogs, in particular, playing is also a way to learn to live in a group, and to slowly find out which position they will have within the pack.

Our pet dogs no longer live according to the harsh laws of nature. This allows them to remain playful to an old age. The only reason for dogs to live in a pack is because this increases their chances of success when hunting.

If they would constantly fight to determine or confirm their position in the hierarchy, there would be a lot of casualties and an injured animal is no help when hunting. We therefore more often see dogs play than fight to establish the hierarchy. After all, their life partly depends on the health of the others in the pack.

When two strange dogs walk past each

other, they will sometimes have a go at each other.

As they are not members of the same pack, this is nothing to do with establishing a hierarchy, but with protecting their territory.

Territory

The territory is the domain of the pack. This territory may be several kilometres across and is divided into three different sectors. In the outer circle of the territory, pack members will make it clear to intruders that they must stay out. If an intruder manages to get into the middle circle, the pack will attack him. However, he will be given the chance to escape during this attack. The innermost circle is the centre of the pack. The puppies stay here and the entire pack retreats to this sector to rest. Defending this place is a matter of life and death. If we look at how closely humans live to each other in the Western world, it is not surprising that dogs have so many territorial conflicts. A dog will, after all, not be satisfied with its own garden.

Its territory is much bigger. The garden is simply the centre of the territory. The rest is outside your garden fence. This means that the territories of dogs which live closely together overlap each other. Even when walking a dog on the lead, it still has a territory. It is a mobile territory, and the dog sees itself as the centre. It is therefore not surprising that two dogs often have a go at each other when taken out for a walk. After all, the centre of the territory must be defended fanatically.

Advice

- Always keep games under control: you determine the course of a game, not your dog.
- When you are playing with your dog, you must be aware that it constantly tries to get over you in the hierarchy. Therefore constantly pay attention to this rule.
  If you think that your dog is trying to dominate the game, stop immediately and ignore it completely for a while.

Don't

- Never let your dog dominate retrieve or tug-of-war games.
- Never let your dog determine how or what you are going to play. That is your decision.

Rule 5

The alpha wins each and every game

When dogs are playing, you can see that a superior animal will always assume a higher position than an inferior animal. The superior animal will decide when the game is over and it will always win.

Advice

Make sure that you always win the last game when playing with your dog. It is possible to let your dog win a game once in a while, but you must dominate the major part of it. How many games your dog is allowed to win depends on the hierarchical relationship between you and your dog. A dominant dog should never be allowed to win. A submissive dog can be allowed to feel like a winner once in a while.

Don't

- Never let your dog win the last game.
- Never finish a retrieve game by throwing the object. The dog will pick up the object and therefore in fact be the winner of the game. A tug-of-war game with a rope must not be finished by letting go of the rope and giving it to the dog. Take the rope and put it away.

Rule 6
Each pack member makes place for the highest in rank.
If a superior animal goes somewhere, all the inferior animals will move out of its way. The superior animal will go in a straight line, without swerving, to the place it wants to go. No other dog will stand in its way. Only inferior animals will move aside.

Don't
- If your dog is coming towards you and wants to move past you, don't move aside.
- Never swerve around your dog if you want to go past it. And don't step over it, even when it is asleep.

Rule 7
The highest in the hierarchy will always go through a narrow passageway first.
A narrow passageway is a very wide term in this context. It is not only a doorway or a gate, but it can also be the alleyway between two houses, the space between parked cars or even a forest path.
The clearest example for this rule is a pack of hunting dogs. When these dogs are let out of their kennel, it is always the animal highest in the hierarchy which exits first. Dogs often run ahead when out on a walk. They do this to confirm their higher position in comparison to their owner.

Advice

- Open a door a little. If your dog wants to go through, close it. Be very careful that your dog's nose doesn't get caught, however! Repeat this until your dog no longer attempts to go through the door. Then go through the door yourself and let your dog follow you.
- Sometimes your dog will try to go ahead of you through a passageway, which cannot be closed with a door or gate. In this case, keep your dog on a four to five metre long lead. Walk towards the passageway. If your dog wants to go ahead, turn around and walk away from the passageway. If your dog doesn't follow straight away, it will get a sudden pull when the lead tightens. It should now follow you. Repeat these steps until your dog no longer shows the intention of going through the passageway first.

Don't

- You must never try to physically prevent a dog from going through a passageway first. There is no point in forcing your dog physically to accept you as a leader. If you try to stop your dog in such a manner, it will soon learn that it simply has to be faster than you.
  This way, the dog tries to prevent you stopping it.
- Never let your dog pull on the lead when walking it.

Rule 8
Each pack member pays respect to the alpha male every day.

All dogs in a pack confirm their submissive position every day by consistently applying the rules of the pack. They devote most of their time to the alpha dog, which they honour. This becomes clear in their greetings, for example. First the highest in the hierarchy is greeted, and then the other members according to their status. Everything that happens in a pack reflects the movement from top to bottom. Inferior animals always respect superior animals.

Advice
- Respect all the rules of the pack every day.
- Always respect the hierarchy.
- Always show respect for those superior (for children, this is the parents).
- When eating, when wiping your feet after a walk or when going through a passageway, make sure that you always come first and that your dog always comes last.
- Always greet the highest members of the hierarchy first, and the lower members after that. This means that a dog must be greeted last.

Don't
- It is absolutely wrong to act against the hierarchy. According to the rules of the pack, a superior animal must never let an inferior animal have an advantage.
  It is therefore very confusing for your dog, if, for example, you greet it before you greet the other members of the family.

Rule 9
The alpha dog decides what's best.
The pack leader decides everything that goes on within a pack. He decides when to sleep, when to hunt, when to play, when to eat, etc. No other dog within the pack will make decisions which contradict those of the leader.

Advice
- As the boss, you make all the decisions for your dog within the human/dog pack. You decide when your dog is allowed to go for a walk, to eat, play and sleep.

Don't
- Never let your dog decide. Therefore do not follow its demand (begging) to go for a walk or to play with it. You alone decide when you do anything with your dog.

Rule 10
An inferior member of the pack pays attention to the alpha.
A superior animal never approaches an inferior animal, unless it wants to reprimand it.
An inferior animal always approaches a superior animal, and assumes a submissive posture (head low, ears back, and tail low). This is called active submission. A superior animal may approach an inferior animal to reprimand it. In this case, the superior animal will assume a superior posture (dominance).

Active submission
Inferior dogs sometimes approach superior dogs. In this case, they assume a low posture: the ears are pinned back, the tail is carried low and the body is

generally held somewhat lower towards the ground. When an inferior animal reaches the superior animal, it will lick the corners of its mouth. This is a social gesture which dogs inherited from their ancestors. With this gesture, the inferior dog confirms the superior dog in its status. We call this active submission: the inferior dog initiates the submission.

Passive submission
In the case of passive submission, the inferior animal also assumes a low posture. The only difference is that this time the superior animal initiates the submission. When it approaches the inferior animal with a superior posture, the inferior animal will react immediately and assume an inferior posture. If it does not do this, it will be reprimanded by the superior animal.

Advice
• Always make your dog approach you.
• Regularly play chase games, where your dog must follow you.
• Only ever approach your dog when you need to reprimand it.

Don't
• Never approach your dog. Particularly not when it is lying in its safe place. The dog wants to have some peace and quiet here. When approaching your dog, you are moving for it and a superior animal never moves for an inferior animal!

Rule 11
Only the alpha animal has the right to ignore.
A superior animal will often ignore the inferior animal when it passes by. An inferior animal would never dare to ignore a superior dog in such a way, it would be punished immediately. In general, a pack leader will usually ignore the lowest members of the pack.
It is also not his job to watch over the entire pack, as this would require far too much

energy. Every member of the pack therefore needs to pay attention to the alpha animal. The group thus stays together: where the alpha animal leads, the rest follow.

Advice
• Regularly ignore your dog when passing by.
  This shows it that you are still higher up in the hierarchy.
• When your dog is importunately demanding your attention or jumping up at you, it is best to ignore it completely. Ignoring it is punishment for your dog. Dogs would rather have negative attention than no attention at all. If you shout at your dog for jumping up at you, you are actually paying attention to it, which is exactly what it wants.

Don't
• Never let your dog ignore you. If necessary, demand its attention or motivate it so that it becomes interested in you again.

Rule 12
A superior animal has
the right to allow privileges.
Both with humans and with dogs, we often see that someone who is high up in the hierarchy often deals out privileges to the ones directly below. The lower animal can in turn hand out privileges to the one below it. An animal will never hand out more privileges than it received. This means that the lowest animal in the hierarchy will have the least privileges of all. Privileges which have been handed out can also be withdrawn. If an animal doesn't behave exceptionally well, it could easily lose all its privileges.

Advice
• Once you have established the hierarchy within your human/dog pack with the help of the above rules, you can give your dog some privileges. In other words: you may decide to apply some of the rules less strictly. You need to realize that such privileges allow your dog to move a little closer to the rest of the family in terms of hierarchy. Therefore never give your dog too much freedom. Make sure that there is still enough distance in the hierarchy between your dog and the rest of the family.
• You may hand out privileges, but you don't have to!

Don't

• Never allow a dog privileges that are not far enough below those of all the other members of the pack. It will soon take advantage.

(Dis)obedience

A dog that won't obey you is not just a problem for you, but also for your surroundings. It's therefore important to avoid unwanted behaviour. In fact, this is what training your dog is all about, so get started early. Once again, *Start 'em young!* should be your motto.

An untrained dog is not just a nuisance, but can also cause dangerous situations by running into the road, chasing joggers or jumping at people. A dog must be trained out of this undesirable behaviour as quickly as possible. The longer you let it go on, the more difficult it will become to correct. The best thing to do is to attend a special obedience course. This won't only help to correct the dog's behaviour, but its owner also learns how to handle undesirable behaviour at home. A dog must not only obey its master during training, but at home too.

Always be consistent when training good behaviour and correcting annoying behaviour. This means a dog may always behave in a certain way, or must never behave that way. Reward it for good behaviour and never punish it after the event for any wrongdoing. If your dog finally comes after you've been calling it for a long time, then reward it. If you're angry because you had to wait so long, it may feel it's actually being punished for coming. It will probably not obey at all next time for fear of punishment.

Try to take no notice of undesirable behaviour. Your dog will perceive your reaction (even a negative one) as a reward for this behaviour. If you need to correct your dog, then do this immediately. Use your voice or grip it by the scruff of its neck and push it to the ground. This is the way a mother dog calls her pups to order. Rewards for good behaviour are, by far, preferable to punishment; they always achieve a better result.

House-training

The very first training and one of the most important that a dog needs is house-training. The basis for good house-training is keeping a good eye on your puppy. If you pay attention, you will notice that it will sniff a long time and turn around a certain spot before doing its business there. Pick it up gently and place it outside, always at the same place. Reward it abundantly if it does its business there.

Another good moment for house-training is after eating or sleeping. A puppy often needs to do its business at these times. Let it relieve itself before playing with it, otherwise it will forget to do so and you'll not reach your goal. For the first few days, take your puppy out for a walk just after it's eaten or woken up. It will quickly learn the meaning, especially if it's rewarded with a dog biscuit for a successful attempt.

Of course, it's not always possible to go out after every snack or snooze. Lay newspapers at different spots in the house. Whenever the pup needs to do its business, place it on a newspaper. After some time it will start to look for a place itself. Then start to reduce the number of newspapers until there is just one left, at the front or back door. The puppy will learn to go to the door if it needs to relieve itself. Then you put it on the lead and go out with it. Finally you can remove the last newspaper. Your puppy is now house-trained.

One thing that certainly won't work is punishing an accident after the event. A dog whose nose is rubbed in its urine or its stools won't understand that at all. It will only get frightened of you. Rewarding works much better than punishment.

An indoor kennel or cage can be a good tool to help in house-training. A puppy won't foul its own nest, so a kennel can be a good solution for the night, or during periods in the day when you can't watch it. But a kennel must not become a prison where your dog is locked up day and night.

First exercises

The basic commands for an obedient dog are those for *sit, lie down, come* and *stay*. You can teach a pup *to sit* by holding a piece of dog biscuit above its nose and then slowly moving it backwards. The puppy's head will also move backwards until its hind legs slowly go down. At that moment you call "Sit!". After a few attempts, it will quickly know this nice game. Use the "Sit!" command before you give your dog its food, put it on the lead, or before it's allowed to cross the street.

Teaching the command *to lie down* is similar. Instead of moving the piece of dog biscuit backwards, move it down vertically until your hand reaches the ground and then forwards. The dog will also move its forepaws forwards and lie down on its own. At that moment call "Lie down!" or "Lay!". This command is useful when you want a dog to be quiet.

Two people are needed for the "Come!" command. One holds the dog back while the other runs away. After about fifteen metres, he stops and enthusiastically calls "Come!". The other person now lets the dog free, and it should obey the command at once. Again you reward it abundantly. The "Come!" command is useful in many situations and good for safety too.

A dog learns *to stay* from the sitting or lying position. While it's sitting or lying down, you call the command "Stay!" and then step back one step. If the dog moves with you, quietly put it back in position, without displaying anger. If you do react angrily, you're actually punishing it for coming to you, and you'll only confuse your dog. It can't understand that coming is rewarded one time, and punished another. Once the dog stays nicely, reward it abundantly. Practise this exercise with increasing distances, at first no more than one metre. The "Stay!" command is useful when getting out of the car.

Courses
Obedience courses to help you bring up your dog are available across the country. These courses are not just informative, but also fun for dog and master. With a puppy, you can begin with a puppy course. This is designed to provide the basic training. A puppy that has attended such a course has learned about all kinds of things that it will confront in later life: other dogs, humans, traffic and others. The puppy will also learn obedience and to follow a number of basic commands. Apart from all that, attention will be given to important subjects such as brushing, being alone, travelling in a car, and doing its business in the right places.

The next step after a puppy course is a course for young dogs. This course repeats the basic exercises and ensures that the growing dog doesn't get into bad habits. After this, the dog can move on to an obedience course for full-grown dogs.

For more information on where to find courses in your area, contact your local kennel club. You can get its address from The Kennel Club of Great Britain in London. In some areas, the RSPCA organises obedience classes and your local branch may be able to give you information.

Play and toys

There are various ways to play with your dog. You can romp and run with it, but also play a number of games, such as retrieving, tug-of-war, hide-and-seek and catch. A dummy is ideal for retrieving, and you can play tug-of-war with an old sock or a special tugging rope. Start with tug-of-war only when your dog is a year old. A puppy must first get its second teeth and then they need several months to strengthen. There's a real chance of your dog's teeth becoming deformed if it starts playing tug-of-war too soon. You can use almost anything for a game of hide-and-seek. Never use too small a ball for games. It can easily get lodged into the dog's throat.

Play is extremely important. Not only does it strengthen the bond between dog and master, but it's also healthy for both. Make sure that you're the one that ends the game. Only stop when the dog has brought back the ball or frisbee, and make sure you always win the tug-of-war. This confirms your dominant position in the hierarchy. Use these toys only during play, so that the dog doesn't forget their significance.

When choosing a special dog toy, remember that dogs are hardly careful with them. So always buy toys of good quality, which a dog can't easily destroy. Be very careful with sticks and twigs. The latter, particularly, can easily splinter. A splinter of wood in your dog's throat or intestines can cause awful problems. Throwing sticks or twigs can also be dangerous. If they stick into the ground, a dog can easily run into them with an open mouth.

Aggression

Yorkshire terriers and Australian Silky terriers are not normally aggressive. It can happen, however, that they are less friendly towards other animals or people. It is therefore good to know a bit more about aggressive behaviour in dogs.

There are two different types of aggressive behaviour in dogs: The anxious-aggressive dog and the dominant-aggressive dog. An anxious-aggressive dog can be recognised by its pulled-back ears and its lowly held tail. It will have pulled in its lips, baring its teeth. This dog is aggressive because it's very frightened and feels cornered. It would prefer to run away, but if it can't then it will bite to defend itself. It will grab its victim anywhere it can. The attack is usually brief and, as soon as the dog can see a way to escape, it's gone. In a confrontation with other dogs, it will normally turn out as the loser. It can become more aggressive once it's recognised that people or other dogs are afraid of it. If you try to correct this behaviour, you first have to try to understand what the dog is afraid of. Professional advice is a good idea here, as the wrong approach can easily make the problem worse.

The dominant-aggressive dog's body language is different. Its ears are pricked and its tail is raised and stiff. This dog will go only for its victim's arms, legs or throat. It is self-assured and highly placed in the dog hierarchy. Its attack is a display of power rather than a consequence of fear. This dog needs to know who the boss is. You must bring it up rigorously and with a strong hand. An obedience course can help.

A dog may also bite when in pain. This is a natural defensive reaction. In this case try to resolve the dog's fear as far as possible. Reward it for letting you get to the painful spot. Be careful, because a dog in pain may also bite its master! Muzzling it can help prevent problems if you have to do something that may be painful. Never punish a dog for this type of aggression!

Socialisation

If your dog behaves in a timid manner, the reason for this behaviour can usually be found in the first few weeks of its life. A lack of new experiences in this very important so-called socialisation phase has a big influence on the adult dog's behaviour. If a dog does not get to see humans, other dogs or other animals during this phase, it will be distant later. This distance is common with dogs that have grown up in a barn or kennel, with very little human contact. As mentioned above, fear can lead to aggression. It is very important that the dog gets as many new experiences as possible during its first few weeks. Take it into town in the car or on the bus, walk down a busy street with it and let it have a lot of contact with people, other dogs and other animals.

It's a huge task to turn an anxious, poorly socialised dog into a real pet. It will probably take an enormous amount of attention, love, patience and energy to get such an animal used to everything around it. Reward it often and give it plenty of time to adapt and, over time, it will learn to trust you and become less anxious. Try not to force anything, because that will always have the reverse effect. Here too, an obedience class can help a lot.

Dogs are often frightened of strangers. Have visitors give it something tasty as a treat. Put a can of dog biscuits by the door, so that your visitors can spoil your dog when they arrive. Here again, don't try to force anything. If the dog is still frightened, leave it in peace.

Dogs are often frightened in certain situations; well-known examples are thunderstorms and fireworks. In these cases try to ignore your dog's anxious behaviour. If you react to its whimpering and whining, it's the same as rewarding it. If you ignore its fear completely, the dog will quickly learn that nothing is wrong. You can speed up this learning process by rewarding its positive behaviour.

Rewarding

Rewarding forms the basis for bringing up a dog. Rewarding good behaviour works far better than punishing bad behaviour and rewarding is also much more fun. Over time the opinions on how to bring up dogs have gradually changed. In the past, a sharp pull on the lead was considered the appropriate way to correct bad behaviour. Today, experts view rewards as a positive incentive to get dogs to do what we expect of them.

There are many ways of rewarding a dog. The usual ways are a pat or a friendly word, even without a tasty treat to go with it. When bringing up a puppy, a tasty treat at the right moment will do wonders, though. Make sure that you always have something tasty in your pocket to reward it for good behaviour.

Another form of reward is play. Whenever a dog notices that you have a ball in your pocket, it won't go far from your side. As soon as you've finished playing, put the ball away. This way your dog will always do its best in exchange for a game.

Despite the emphasis you put on rewarding good behaviour, a dog can sometimes be a nuisance or disobedient. You must correct such behaviour immediately. Always be consistent: once "no" must always mean "no".

Barking

Dogs that bark too much and too often are a nuisance for their surroundings. A dog owner may tolerate barking up to a point, but neighbours are often annoyed by the unnecessary noise. Don't encourage your puppy to bark and yelp. Of course, it should be able to announce its presence, but if it goes on barking it must be called to order with a strict "Quiet!". If your puppy does not listen, you can gently hold its muzzle closed with your hand.

A dog will sometimes bark for long periods when left alone. It feels threatened and tries to get someone's attention by barking. There are special training programmes for this problem, where a dog learns that being alone is nothing to be afraid of, and that its master will always return.

You can practise this with your dog at home. Leave the room and come back in at once. Reward your dog if it stays quiet. Gradually increase the length of your absences and keep rewarding it as long as it remains quiet. Never punish your dog if it does bark or yelp. It will never understand punishment afterwards, and this will only make the problem worse. Never go back into the room as long as your dog is barking, as it will view this as a reward.

You might want to make the dog feel more comfortable by switching the radio on for company during your absence. It will eventually learn that you always come back and the barking will reduce. If you don't get the required result, attend an obedience course.

Breeding

Dogs, and thus also Yorkies and Silkies, follow their instincts, and reproduction is one of nature's most important processes. For people who enjoy breeding dogs this is positive.

Those who simply want a cosy companion however, will miss the regular adventures with females on heat and unrestrainable males like toothache. But knowing a little about canine reproduction will help you to understand why they behave the way they do, and what measures you need to take when this happens.

Liability

Breeding dogs is much more than simply 1+1= many. If you're planning to breed with your terrier, be on your guard. The whole affair can quite easily turn into a financial disaster, because, under the law, a breeder is liable for the quality of his puppies.

The kennel clubs place strict conditions on animals used for breeding. They need to be tested for certain hereditary abnormalities (see the chapter *Health*). By doing this, a breeder shows that he cares. If you breed a litter of puppies and sell them without having had these tests done, you can be held liable by the new owners for any costs arising from any inherited defects. These veterinary costs can be enormous! So contact a breed club if you plan to breed a litter of puppies.

The female in season

Bitches become sexually mature at about eight to twelve months. Then they go into season for the first time. They are on heat for two to three weeks. During this period they discharge little drops of blood and they are very attractive to males. The bitch is fertile during the second half of her season, and will accept a male to mate. The best time for mating is between the ninth and thirteenth day of her season. A female's first season is often shorter and less severe than those that follow. If you do want to breed with your bitch, you must allow the first and the second season to pass. Most bitches go into season twice per year.

If you plan to breed with your terrier in the future, then spaying is not an option to prevent unwanted offspring. A temporary solution is a contraceptive injection, although this is controversial because of side effects such as womb infections.

Phantom pregnancy

A phantom pregnancy is a not uncommon occurrence. The female behaves as if she has a litter. She takes all kinds of things to her basket and treats them like puppies. Her milk teats swell up and sometimes milk is actually produced. The female will sometimes behave aggressively towards people or other animals, as if she is defending her young.

Phantom pregnancies usually begin two months after a season and can last a number of weeks. If it happens to a bitch once, it will often re-occur after every season. If this is a problem, spaying is the best solution, because continual phantom pregnancies increase the risk of womb or teat conditions. Spaying can, however, influence the coat structure, which will make the hair prone to becoming tangled more easily.

In the short term a hormone treatment is worth trying, perhaps also homeopathic medicines. Camphor can give relief when teats are heavily swollen, but rubbing the teats with ice or a cold cloth (moisten and freeze) can also help relieve the pain. Feed the female less than usual, and make sure she gets enough distraction and extra exercise.

Preparing to breed

If you do plan to breed a litter of puppies, you must first wait for your female to be physically and mentally fully grown. In any event you must wait until her third season. To mate a bitch, you need a male. You could simply let her out on the street and she would quickly return home pregnant. But if you have a purebred Yorkie or Silky, then it certainly makes sense to mate her with the best possible candidate, even if she does not have a pedigree. Be meticulous with your preparations. Think especially about the following: Accompanying a bitch through pregnancy, birth and the first eight to twelve weeks afterwards is a time-consuming affair. Never breed with dogs that have congenital defects, and the same applies to dogs without papers! The same goes for hyperactive, nervous and shy dogs.

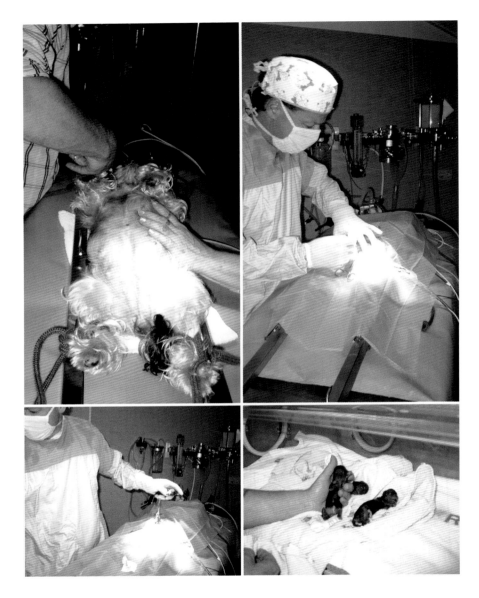

Giving birth is not always that easy. Sometimes the vet will have to intervene and perform a caesarean.

Left above: the young mother is safely tight to the surgeons table and has been given anaesthetics.

Right above: the incision is made.

Left below: the vet takes a pup with its afterbirth out.

Right below: the pups are recovering in the incubator. The pups must be dried very well. Rubbing them stimulates the blood circulation and their breathing.

If your dog does have a pedigree, then mate her with a dog that also has one. For more information, contact the breed association. You will find the addresses in the chapter *Breed Associations*.

Pregnancy

It's often difficult to tell at first if a bitch is pregnant. Only after about four weeks can you feel the pups in her belly. She will now slowly become fatter and her behaviour will usually change. Her teats will swell up during the last few weeks of pregnancy.

The average pregnancy lasts 63 days, and costs the bitch more and more in terms of energy.
In the beginning she should be fed her normal amount of food, but her nutritional needs increase in jumps during the second half of the pregnancy. Give her approximately fifteen percent more food each week from the fifth week on. The mother-to-be needs extra energy and proteins during this phase of her pregnancy. During the last weeks you can give her a concentrated food, which is rich in energy, such as dry puppy food. Divide this into several small portions per day, as she can no longer deal with large portions of food. Towards the end of the pregnancy, her energy needs can easily be one-and-a-half times more than usual.

After about seven weeks, the mother will start to demonstrate nesting behaviour and to look for a place to give birth to her young. This might be her own basket or a special birthing box. This must be ready at least a week before the birth to give the mother time to get used to it. The basket or box should preferably be in a quiet place.

Birth

The average litter counts three to five puppies. The birth normally takes place without too many problems. If you are in any doubt, you must contact your vet straight away, of course!
Yorkshire terrier puppies are born with smooth hair. They are black with some rust-brown (tan) markings. The colour normally changes at the age of approximately three to six months, but it can be as late as twelve to eighteen months. At the age of two to three years, the coat will have its final colour. The colour change starts on the head, which lightens up to a slate-blue and finally gets its end-colour. If your puppies are the right colour too early, they will probably become too

light over time. Silky terriers are born completely black and with smooth hair. In the case of the Silky, too, the colour changes progressively.

Suckling and weaning

A few days before giving birth the mother-to-be will be most willing to present her belly when you stroke it softly. This is the moment to shorten the long hair on her belly. It must be easy for the pups to reach the milk and this also makes it easier for you to keep the mother clean. After giving birth, the bitch starts to produce milk. The suckling period is very demanding. During the first three to four weeks the pups rely entirely on their mother's milk. During this time she needs extra food and fluids. This can be up to three or four times the normal amount. If she's producing too little milk, you can give both the mother and her young special puppy milk.

Here too, divide the high quantity of food the mother needs into several smaller portions. Again, choose a concentrated, high-energy, food and give her plenty of fresh drinking water. Do not give the bitch cow's milk, as this can cause diarrhoea.

You can give the puppies some supplemental solid food when they are three to four weeks old. There are special puppy foods available that follow on well from the mother's milk and can easily be eaten with their milk teeth.

Ideally, the puppies are fully weaned at an age of six to seven weeks, i.e. they no longer drink their mother's milk. The mother's milk production gradually stops and her food needs also drop. Within a few weeks after weaning, the mother should be back to getting the same amount of food as before the pregnancy.

Neutering and spaying

As soon as you are sure that your bitch should never bear a litter spaying is the best solution. During spaying the uterus and the ovaries are surgically removed. The bitch no longer goes into season and can never become pregnant. The best age for spaying is about eighteen months, when the bitch is more or less fully grown.

A male dog may also be neutered for medical reasons or to correct undesirable sexual behaviour. During neutering the testicles are removed, which is a simple procedure and usually without complications. There is no special age for neutering but, where possible, wait until the dog is fully grown. Vasectomy is sufficient where it's only a case of making the dog infertile. In this case the dog keeps its sexual drive but can no longer reproduce.

Of course, neutering and spaying change the hormone levels. This can even influence the coat structure. In the case of some breeds, the hairs lose their outer layer, which makes them shine, and they become totally dry and dull. The coat might tangle up more easily and can even become totally matted. Before deciding to have your dog spayed or neutered, get plenty of information from your vet.

Shows

Visiting a show is highly recommended if you want to learn more about a certain breed. You will also be able to get into direct contact with breeders and other owners.

Showing animals is a very competitive sport, which breeders and exhibitors invest a lot of time in. Some breeders even dedicate their life to this. There are many things to be considered. You need to choose which shows to enter and what you need to achieve for the dog to be awarded a title. The entry forms, payments, hotel reservations, everything needs to be taken care of well in advance. If you want to make a good appearance in the ring with your dog, you should also find appropriate clothing for yourself.

Of course, the most important thing is your dog. Showing a dog requires a lot of preparation. You cannot simply start preparing your dog a few weeks before the show, but you must start to prepare it for a show career when it is very young, as it takes a lot of training until a dog presents itself well.

For some breeds, many dogs compete in the classes, and this will make it a lot more difficult to win a title. Sometimes, the representative of a very rare breed may be crowned Champion, without the dog ever having competed against another one of its kind. It's also possible for the judge to withhold the award. In order to become Champion your dog needs to have three Challenge Certificates awarded by three different judges. Of those three, at least one should be achieved when the dog is twelve months or older. Challenge

Certificates can also be awarded to the best of each sex in a breed. The British system allows a certain number of dogs per breed to be awarded the Challenge Certificate. The annual limit of Challenge Certificates to be awarded to representatives of a certain breed may be 30 or just 6.

When the dogs enter the ring, the judge looks at them very carefully. Each dog is examined visually and by hand. The breed standards of many dog breeds contain remarks regarding the build. The teeth will also be examined, as each breed standard will have its own notes regarding an undershot jaw or scissor bite. It is understandable that the judge will need to feel the dog in order to fully compare it to the breed standard. The breed standards also contain notes on the gait and movement, which is why the judge will also need to see your dog move. Judges also pay attention to the way a dog carries its head and tail.

Ring craft classes

Here you are taught how best to prepare your dog for a show and how to present it when the big day has finally arrived, so that it makes the best possible impression in the ring and with the judge. It is a good idea to first visit a show as a spectator, so that you know the procedure of a show.

There are usually several classes, e.g. one for puppies and one for more experienced dogs. The classes are usually very sociable events, where training is combined with lots of fun. It is not easy to teach a dog all the tricks of showing. Even if you don't plan to follow a showing career with your dog, it is still a good idea to take it to a course. Your dog will learn to socialize with people other than its master and with other dogs. It will also learn to walk on the lead properly without being distracted.

Some clubs which organise ring craft classes also organise friendly unofficial shows and Companion Dog Shows for their members once in a while.

Dog Clubs

There is a large number of dog clubs in the UK. For more information, look on the site of The Kennel Club, and click on the Breed Standard button.

Types of Shows

There are different types of shows, of which we will give a very brief overview here.
- Single Breed Shows (for one breed only, organised by a breed club)
- Companion Dog Shows (for charitable causes)
- Open Shows (you can qualify for Crufts at some of these shows)
- Championship Shows (the most prestigious shows, often the possibility to qualify for Crufts and to attain Challenge Certificates).

Getting ready for a show

Of course, your dog needs to be in perfect condition for a show. The judge will not be impressed if your dog's coat is dirty or tangled or if its paws are muddy. Be aware: the work to present a show quality dog starts several months before the actual show. Once you've started, you must keep the coat in a good condition every day. It's a good idea to let an experienced dog groom or breeder show you how to get your dog ready for a show. Especially with the long coats of Yorkies and Silkies, it is very important to do this properly. You can quite easily mess things up with your dog's coat, and it takes quite a while for it to grow back to full length. The nails must be cut properly and the teeth need to be free of tartar. Your dog must not be suffering from any parasites or diseases. Judges also don't like dogs that are badly brought up, timid or nervous.

Of course, your dog must look very smart for the show. The judge will not be impressed if its coat is not clean, and its paws are dirty. The dog must also be free of parasites and ailments. Apart from those things, judges also hate badly brought-up, anxious or nervous dogs. Get in touch with your local dog club or the breed association if you want to know more about shows.
If you have any more questions about dog shows, you can contact your local breed association or kennel club.

Don't forget!

If you're planning to take your dog to a club match or in fact to any show, you need to be well prepared. Don't forget the following:

For yourself:
- Show documents if they have been sent to you
- Food and drink
- Clip for the catalogue number
- Chairs if an outdoor show

For your dog:
- Food and water bowls and food
- Dog blanket and perhaps a cushion
- Show lead
- Grooming equipment
- A benching chain and collar

Parasites

All dogs are vulnerable to various sorts of parasites. Parasites are tiny creatures that live at the expense of another animal. They feed on blood, skin and other body substances. There are two main types. Internal parasites live within their host animal's body (tapeworm and roundworm for example) and external parasites live on the animal's exterior, usually in its coat (fleas and ticks), but also in its ears (ear mite).

Fleas

Fleas feed on a dog's blood. They cause not only itching and skin problems, but can also carry infections such as tapeworm. In large numbers they can cause anaemia and dogs can also become allergic to a flea's saliva, which can cause serious skin conditions.
So it's important that you treat your dog for fleas as effectively as possible. Do not just treat the animal itself, but also its surroundings.

For treatment of the dog, there are various medicines: drops for the neck and to put in its food, flea collars, long-life sprays and flea powders. There are various sprays in pet shops, which can be used to eradicate fleas in the dog's immediate surroundings. Choose a spray that kills both adult fleas and their larvae. If your dog goes in your car, you should spray that too.

Fleas can also affect other pets, so you should treat those too. When spraying a room, cover any aquarium or fishbowl. If the spray reaches the water, it can be fatal for your fish! Your vet and pet shop have a wide range of flea treatments and can advise you on the subject.

Ticks

Ticks are small, spider-like parasites. They feed on the blood of the animal or person they've settled on. A tick looks like a tiny, grey-coloured leather bag with eight feet. When it has sucked itself full, it can easily be five to ten times its own size and is darker in colour. Dogs usually fall victim to ticks in bushes, woods or long grass. Ticks cause not only irritation by their blood-sucking, but can also carry a number of serious diseases. This applies especially to the Mediterranean countries, were ticks can be infected with blood parasites. In our country these diseases are fortunately less common, but Lyme disease, which can also affect humans, has reached our shores. Your vet can prescribe a special treatment if you're planning to take your dog to southern Europe. It is important to fight ticks as effectively as possible. Check your dog regularly, especially when it's been running free in woods and bushes. It can also wear an anti-tick collar.

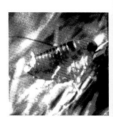

Flea

Removing a tick is simple using tick tweezers. Grip the tick with the tweezers, very close to the dog's skin, and carefully pull it out. You can also grip the tick between your fingers and pull it carefully out. You must disinfect the spot where the tick had been, using iodine to prevent infection. Never soak the tick in alcohol, ether or oil. In a shock reaction the tick may discharge the infected contents of its stomach into the dog's skin.

Tick

Worms

Dogs can suffer from various types of worms. The most common are tapeworm and roundworm. Tapeworm causes diarrhoea and poor general condition. With a tapeworm infection you can sometimes find small pieces of the worm around the dog's anus or on its bed. In this case, the dog must be wormed. You should also check your dog for fleas, as these can carry the tapeworm infection.

Tapeworm

Roundworm is a condition that reoccurs regularly. Puppies are often infected by their mother's milk. Roundworm causes problems, such as diarrhoea, loss of weight and stagnated growth, particularly in younger dogs. In serious cases the pup becomes thin, but with a swollen belly. It may vomit and you can then see the worms in its vomit. They are spaghetti-like tendrils. In its first year, a puppy needs to be treated every three months with a worm treatment. Adult dogs should be treated every six months.

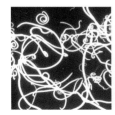

Roundworm

Health

Here we go into all the medical ups and downs of Yorkshire terriers and Australian Silky terriers. We will, however, give you some information about illnesses and abnormalities which are more common to this breed than to others.

Patella luxation

In the case of this abnormality, the kneecap is not placed centrally at the end of the shinbone. The kneecap ends up next to the joint. A luxating kneecap can occur if the groove of the femur is not deep enough. This can be hereditary, but it can also be the result of trauma (an accident). In this case the luxation will be combined with ruptured ligaments. Luxation occurs in different severities. The amount of pain and discomfort varies per dog. If the luxation is of minor gradation, it can be sufficient to move the attachment of the knee tendon. If the groove of the femur is not deep enough, it must be deepened. Nowadays, techniques are chosen which save the cartilage. The joint can be made tighter in order to keep the kneecap in its position more securely.

Slippery floors and strange movements (such as running after balls too wildly, bouncing and quick turns) are not healthy for the joints of any dogs, whether they are big or small, puppies or adults.

Knee

Schematic representation of the knee

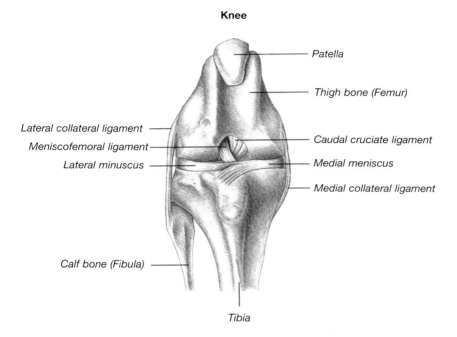

- Patella
- Thigh bone (Femur)
- Caudal cruciate ligament
- Medial meniscus
- Medial collateral ligament

Lateral collateral ligament —
Meniscofemoral ligament —
Lateral minuscus —

Calf bone (Fibula) —

Tibia

Eye conditions

Cross-sectional view of the eye

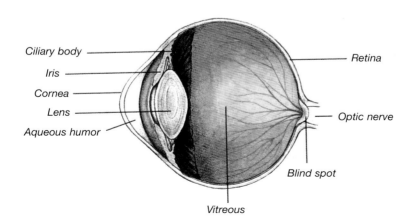

Ciliary body —
Iris —
Cornea —
Lens —
Aqueous humor —

- Retina
- Optic nerve
- Blind spot

Vitreous

Progressive Retina Atrophy (PRA)

PRA is a degenerative condition of the retina and will eventually result in blindness. In the beginning, the dog will have full sight in the daylight until it is approximately five years old. It will become totally blind between five and nine years of age.

Left:

normal retina

Right:

PRA

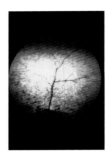

Cataracts

Dogs are examined for cataracts at the same time as for PRA. This condition is caused by a clouding of the retina and gives a blurry vision. It can occur at a young age and it is passed on by both parent animals. If only part of the retina is affected, cataracts need not lead to total blindness. Unfortunately they usually do, however.

Left:

early stage cataract

Right:

advanced stage cataract

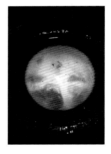

Entropion and ectropion

These are hereditary conditions of the eyelids. In the case of entropion, the eyelid curls to the inside, in the case of ectropion to the outside. With entropion the eyelashes will come in contact with the eyeball, which will result in irritation and red watering eyes. The eyes will become inflamed and discharge pus. This can lead to serious damage to the cornea and eventually to blindness. Entropion and ectropion can be corrected surgically. Breeding with a dog which has (had) ectropion or entropion is inadvisable.

Entropion

Diseases caused by viruses and other organisms

Pseudo rabies

Pseudo rabies or Aujeszky's disease is actually a disease found in pigs. The virus is transferred to other animals when they eat raw pork which is infected. The disease affects the central nervous system. A dog which has been infected with the virus becomes restless, apathetic, nervous and loses its appetite. Aujeszky's disease progresses incredibly quickly: the animal will become paralysed and die within a week. There is no cure. Therefore never feed dogs or other pets raw or not properly cooked pork.

Corona

Corona is a viral disease, the symptoms of which are vomiting and diarrhoea. This disease looks like a parvovirus infection, but is less severe in its progress. Besides the symptoms listed under parvovirus, other symptoms include damage to the mucous membranes, which manifests itself in eye and nose discharge. The disease is spread via faeces.

Hepatitis

Hepatitis is a highly infectious liver disease. The virus is found in both dogs and foxes. The noticeable symptoms vary widely. Approximately a week after infection, the body temperature increases, after which the animal's temperature starts to fluctuate.

The dog remains lively during the first few days, but this changes. Symptoms include: coughing and an inflamed throat, moist eyes, lack of appetite, sometimes in combination with vomiting and/or diarrhoea. The dog's eyes will cloud over. The virus is spread via the urine of infected dogs. As infected dogs urinate in parks and against trees, the disease spreads very quickly.

Hepatitis symptoms vary from light fever to a very serious liver infection. If the disease is treated at an early stage, there is a chance of full recovery. If the liver is infected, the fever will run very high and Invariably, if the disease reaches this stage the dog will die. Hepatitis can cause young dogs and puppies to die very suddenly. Hepatitis is not always easy to diagnose, as the symptoms are very similar to those of Carré's disease.

Carré's disease

This disease is caused by a virus and is highly infectious. The severity of the first symptoms, a runny nose and some coughing, is often underestimated.

Shortly after that, fever, lack of appetite, vomiting and/or diarrhoea follows. Furthermore, the dog will suffer from an inflamed throat and pussy discharge from the nose and eyes, spasms and cramps. A young dog may suddenly become severely ill. The virus causes inflammation in the intestines, but also meningitis. Many dogs do not survive this disease. The dogs that do survive often suffer permanent nerve damage or a tick. Many dogs have behavioural disorders which they did not have before the infection, e.g. orientation problems. The disease is spread via saliva, urine and faeces.

Rabies
This viral disease is fatal to humans and dogs. The virus enters the body when saliva from an infected animal reaches a wound on a hitherto healthy animal. It spreads via nerves to the brain, and will eventually kill the animal. After being bitten by an infected animal, it can take up to 50 days before the new victim shows any symptoms. The final phase of this disease is terrible.
The brain is affected by the virus, the dog is terrified, hides in a corner, and its behaviour can suddenly switch, i.e. the sweetest dog may suddenly become feral and very aggressive. It will bite everything and attack anything that comes close to it. Luckily, rabies does not exist in the UK, but if you are planning to take your dog abroad, you should have it vaccinated. Rabies is spread via the saliva (bites) of foxes, badgers and other animals.

Kennel cough
The kennel cough syndrome is caused by a number of different micro-organisms: para-influenza virus, Bordetella and others. The disease usually spreads where many dogs are kept closely together, such as in a kennel, dog hotel, at a show or at dog schools. The symptoms of this respiratory problem are a harsh, rough cough and occasionally damage to the lungs.
Dogs do not usually become severely ill from kennel cough, but you must have your dog treated by a vet. Cough medicine (thyme syrup) can help to soften the mucous membranes and a holiday to a place with lots of fresh air can do

wonders. If you are going to leave your dog in a boarding kennel, it is best and usually also required to have your dog vaccinated against kennel cough. You should have your dog vaccinated against this obnoxious cough approximately four weeks before it goes to kennels. The disease is spread via the breath.

Parvovirus

Parvo is a highly infectious viral disease. A dog infected with the parvovirus will not usually survive. The virus is spread via the faeces of an infected dog. When a healthy dog sniffs at these faeces, it becomes infected straight away. The virus penetrates to the intestines, where it causes serious inflammation. Within a very short time, the dog will suffer bloody diarrhoea, may vomit blood, become drowsy, develop a fever and become very seriously ill.
The dog will usually also not eat or drink and can therefore dehydrate.

Treatment primarily consists of administering large amounts of fluid intravenously. Most dogs die within 48 hours after the first symptoms. In puppies, an infection with parvovirus can cause cardiac arrest. Nowadays, puppies are usually vaccinated against parvo virus very early in life. Puppies which have survived the disease may unfortunately die very suddenly later on due to angina.

Weil's disease

Weil's disease (leptospirosis) is a disease caused by micro-organisms. Dogs are most commonly infected in spring or autumn. In younger dogs, the disease can easily be fatal. Humans can also be infected through dogs or rats. A dog swimming in contaminated water might contract bacteria via the mucous membranes or tiny wounds on the skin. The bacteria gather in the liver and kidneys. The symptoms include: high fever, drowsiness and muscle pain. Furthermore, the dog suffers from a lack of appetite, vomiting and is very thirsty. The dog may also suffer from nose bleeds, dark urine and sometimes yellow fever. The disease is spread via the urine of infected rats and dogs.

First aid for dogs

When your dog gets injured or ill, the time that passes before professional medical help is available can be crucial. Whatever you do or don't do in this time can save your pet's life.

Bear in mind that the first aid you apply is only intended to gain control over acute emergency situations. Your dog may have suffered internal injuries, which you cannot see. Therefore always take your dog to a veterinarian for examination!

If you are in any doubt about anything, ask your vet for advice. He will certainly understand if you are uncertain about what to do. Applying medical aid to an animal always has one complication: communication with the patient. You cannot explain to a dog that you are trying to help it and lessen its pain. A seriously injured animal is scared and in a lot of pain. It will therefore often try to escape or to attack its helper(s). You must therefore restrain the dog so that you won't be hurt. At the same time, you must make it clear to the animal, through a firm but friendly approach, that you are in control of the situation, but still sympathetic. Keep on talking calmly and frequently address the animal by its name. The tone of your voice and hearing its name will have a calming, relaxing effect. Lay or sit the dog on a table. This makes it more difficult for the animal to escape and, for you, it makes treatment easier.

Not all cases requiring first aid are the same. One situation may be more severe than another and may require quicker intervention. There is a fixed order of treatment, from very severe to less severe. It is therefore very important to stick to this order when treating wounds and conditions: a beautiful support bandage will not do any good if the victim died in the meantime because it couldn't breathe anymore. In the overview below you will see which life functions must be restored first, before you begin with treating the next function.

Order of treatment
1. Respiration
2. Heart function
3. Blood vessels
4. Shock
5. Poisoning
6. Fractures
7. Digestive tract
8. Other injuries

1. Respiration

Together with the heart function, breathing is an animal's most important vital function. By breathing, oxygen is absorbed into the body, which is necessary to allow the organs and tissues to function properly. If an oxygen deficit goes on for too long, the organs and tissues will become damaged very quickly and eventually die off. If respiration stops, the animal is in acute danger. A dog with breathing difficulties often stretches its neck and tries to inhale air with all its might. The mucous membranes of the tongue and the eyes turn blue and the animal will become unconscious after a while. If your dog is lying absolutely still and you cannot see anything on first sight, check the breathing by laying your hand or a few fingers on the chest: you should feel it moving up and down.

If your dog is suffering from breathing difficulties, take it to fresh air immediately. Try to get behind the cause of the breathing difficulties as quickly as possible and eliminate it as soon as you can. Remove any possibly obstructing objects from the neck (collars, flea collars). Check that no objects are stuck in the throat or windpipe. Don't be too careful, as every second counts now! In some cases you can apply a short thrust on the chest and push the object out with the air from the lungs. Applying pressure on the outside of the throat will also sometimes help.

If the dog is choking on water, you need to lift it up by its back legs with the head hanging down. This allows the fluid to drain from the lungs. Then push on the chest a few times to remove the last remaining fluid from the lungs.

If the breathing still doesn't pick up, you will need to apply mouth-to-mouth resuscitation to your dog. Try to take the victim to the veterinarian as quickly as possible. Continuing to apply mouth-to-mouth resuscitation during the journey.

Possible causes of respiratory problems:
- Too little oxygen in the environment (insufficient ventilation, plastic bag, box)
- Water, gas or smoke in the lungs (drowning, carbon monoxide, fire)
- Swallowed objects, swelling of the mucous membranes in the respiratory tract (asthmatic attack, inflammation), swelling of the tongue (wasp sting)
- Restricted throat (collar, flea collar)
- Damage to the diaphragm, broken ribs
- Damaged lungs
- Suffocating on food (through fright) or vomit

Loss of consciousness
A dog can lose its consciousness for a number of reasons. Epilepsy, a heavy blow, brain haemorrhaging and poisoning are some possibilities. Loss of consciousness is always an emergency, in which case you need to act as follows:
- Get someone to notify the vet straight away.
- Lay the dog on its side, as long as you can't detect a wound there, with the paws pointing away from the body. The head needs to lay somewhat higher than the rest of the body.
- Check the pulse. If necessary, apply heart massage.
- Check the respiration. If necessary, apply mouth-to-mouth resuscitation.
- When the dog is breathing, pull its tongue out of its mouth and remove any food remains.
- Don't give the victim food or water.
- Keep the animal warm with a blanket.

2. Heart function

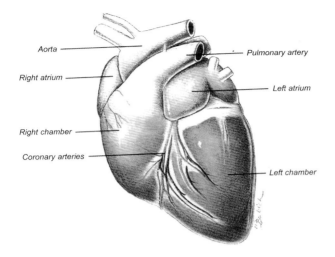

Aorta

Pulmonary artery

Right atrium

Left atrium

Right chamber

Coronary arteries

Left chamber

Above: schematic representation of the heart

Below: cross-sectional view of the heart

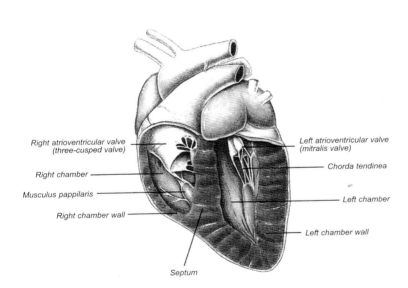

Right atrioventricular valve
(three-cusped valve)

Left atrioventricular valve
(mitralis valve)

Chorda tendinea

Right chamber

Musculus pappilaris

Left chamber

Right chamber wall

Left chamber wall

Septum

A dog can also suffer a heart attack. Not every heart attack results in cardiac arrest.
Some causes of heart attacks include drowning, suffocation, poisoning, severe allergic reaction, trauma or electric shock.
Symptoms include pain, shortness of breath, nausea or vomiting and dizziness.
Don't think that it will pass over. If you suspect heart failure, you must take your dog to the veterinarian as quickly as possible.

3. Blood vessels

Bleeding

A dog can become injured and lose blood. In the case of serious blood loss, the animal may die. How much blood is lost and how quickly depends on the size of the wound, but also on the type of blood vessel. We differentiate between three types of bleeding, depending on the type of blood vessel injured:

Capillary bleeding

This is a fairly harmless bleeding, although it does need to be treated. The wound is not deep (often only a scrape) and there is little loss of blood. Disinfect the wound well. Briefly press it closed with some gauze. You often don't even need to dress it.

Venous bleeding

In this type of bleeding the blood streams out of the wound steadily and is dark red in colour. This is because the blood is flowing towards the heart through the veins and is low in oxygen. Clean the wound well with a disinfectant tissue or sterile gauze soaked in boiled water and then dress it. Take your dog to the veterinarian straight away. He will again disinfect the wound thoroughly and stitch it if necessary.

Arterial bleeding

This is a very serious type of bleeding, which can be fatal for your dog. The blood gushes out of the wound intermittently and is light red in colour. This is because it comes straight from the heart and contains a lot of oxygen. The victim loses a lot of blood in a very short time. You therefore need to act very quickly:
- Hold the dog with a restraining grip and try to calm it. Use your voice to prevent it losing consciousness.
- First check respiration and pulse, and try to stop the bleeding after that.
- Lay the bleeding part of the body higher than the rest of the body.
- Put some sterile gauze or a clean cloth on the wound, and exert pressure with the palm of your hand, so that the blood vessel is squeezed tight. If necessary, put some extra gauze or cotton wool on the wound and exert more pressure. On spots where the skin is loose (lips, cheeks, scruff), tightly push the wound edges together in your fist.
- When the bleeding has stopped, put a thick layer of cotton wool on the gauze or cloth. Bandage the wound with a tight bandage. Keep on exerting pressure.
- Take the animal to the veterinarian as quickly as possible.

Major bleeding at the foot or tail can be stopped by exerting pressure on one of the so-called pressure points with your finger. These are points where the blood vessels run closely under the skin and are easily squeezed tight.

If you cannot manage to stop arterial bleeding in the manner described above, you can apply a tourniquet as a last resort. A tourniquet must never be applied

around the neck or head! After applying a tourniquet, take the victim to the veterinarian as quickly as possible. Be aware that a dog can go into shock as a result of serious bleeding.

Minor cut and stab wounds:
- Hold the victim in a restraining grip. It will probably try to resist.
- Wash your hands thoroughly and use sterile material from a first aid kit as much as possible.
- Remove any hairs that might be in the wound: dampen them with clean water, stroke them out of the wound and cut them off close to the skin. Examine the depth of the wound.
- Rinse the wound clean with a mild disinfectant, which is dissolved in water. You can also dissolve two teaspoons of salt in a litre of tap water. Try to gently rub open small deep stab wounds.
- Wash the skin around the wound with disinfectant shampoo. Cover the wound with sterile gauze, to prevent suds getting in. Rinse with plenty of clean water afterwards.
- With graze wounds, in particular, there may be dirt in the skin. Remove it with a cotton bud or a corner of a clean cloth. Be very careful when doing this!
- Dab the wound dry with a clean, non-fluffy cloth.
- Put disinfectant salve on the wound and bandage it.
- Change the dressing every day and pay close attention to possible wound infections.
- If a scab has formed, you need to prevent the animal removing it. Keep the wound edges supple with Vaseline or cod-liver oil salve.

Major cuts or skin parts missing:
- In these cases your first aid attempts must be directed towards getting the animal to the veterinarian as quickly as possible, and to prevent the situation from worsening.
- The dog might be in a lot of pain. If necessary, apply a restraining grip.
- Remove any big objects, such as splinters, stones and twigs, from the wound. Do not remove objects that have penetrated deeply into the skin. If they stick far out of the wound, cut them off above the skin.
- Soak a clean cloth in a solution of two teaspoons of salt in one litre of water. Lay the wet cloth on the wound and fixate it with tape or bandage clamps.
- Keep the cloth wet with the saline solution during the transport to the veterinarian.
- Make sure that the animal cannot lick or bite at the wound
- A big cut needs to be stitched by a vet within six hours. This will speed up the healing process.

A dog can also encounter wounds when the skin is still intact. Examples of this are bruises or haemorrhages. You can treat these by applying ice cubes which are wrapped in a tea towel. Your dog can also suffer more serious, internal damage. Symptoms include lightening of the mucous membranes and/or bloody discharge of slime from the nose. In the case of internal injuries, you must not move your dog or let it drink: call a vet straight away!

Burns
The skin is a very important organ for any animal. It protects the body against damaging external influences by giving it the right signals (e.g. it is warm,

something is pinching). The skin also sends signals from the animal to its surroundings, e.g. hairs standing up. The coat is covered with aromatic substances. Finally the skin also regulates the body's temperature and the dog's water balance: it makes sure that the body does not dehydrate in a warm environment. Burns can have serious consequences, especially when major parts of the skin have been affected. In these cases the skin can no longer fulfil its vital functions.

In the case of burns you always need to apply first aid. The animal will be in a lot of pain and will need to be examined by a vet as soon as possible. He will judge if the animal can be saved. Whether an animal can recover depends on the percentage of skin damaged and on how deeply the damage penetrates the skin.

You can try to prevent the condition worsening by thoroughly cooling off the animal as quickly as possible. Proceed as follows:
• Cool the burnt part of the skin with cold water as soon as possible, if necessary by dumping the victim in a pond or bucket. The cold not only alleviates the pain, but also gets the warmth out of the skin, which prevents deeper skin layers being seriously damaged.
• You need to cool off the dog for at least ten minutes. Carefully dab dry the area around the affected spot, but don't touch the wound: the risk of infection is too great.
• Don't put any salve or grease on the wound.
• Cover the wound with a clean cloth soaked in a solution of two teaspoons of salt in a litre of water. Keep the cloth damp with this solution during your drive to the veterinarian.
• Give the dog small amounts of water - if it can still swallow - over small time intervals (the mucous membranes of the throat and mouth may have been affected by the smoke).

- Burnt skin can no longer contain the body warmth, which means that the dog may shake because of the cold. Keep it warm with a blanket.
- Even if your dog is obviously in a lot of pain: never feed it painkillers or sedatives of your own accord.

Bite wounds

It can happen that your dog gets bitten by a feral animal, such as a fox or a stray cat or dog. First of all, you should clean the wound with disinfectant. Take your dog to the veterinarian as quickly as possible for further treatment!

4. Shock
Shock

Shock is not actually a condition as such, but can be the result of serious injuries combined with severe blood loss, a bad fright and pain. An injured animal may also become stressed by your attempts to treat it, which can also easily lead to shock. Preventing shock is actually more important than treating it. In the case of shock, too little blood is pumped through the body. If this carries on for long, tissues and organs do not receive enough oxygen. This means that they can die off. If the brain gets insufficient oxygen, the animal will lose consciousness.

In cases where there is a real chance of the dog going into shock, you need to act as follows: Free the respiratory tract by pulling the tongue a little out of the mouth. Check first if there are any objects in the throat or mouth. If necessary, apply mouth-to-mouth resuscitation and/or heart massage and stop any bleeding. An animal with very high fever or heatstroke (sunstroke) needs to be cooled with cold, wet cloths applied to the head and neck. Bring the animal into quiet, dark surroundings. Make sure that the head is positioned a little higher than the rest of the body. In case of shock keep the animal warm with a blanket and maybe with a hot water bottle (maximum 45°C). Alternatively, in the case of sunstroke keep it cool.

If the animal can still drink, give it small amounts of water. Never offer it anything to drink if there is any suspicion of internal damage! Take the animal to the veterinarian as quickly as possible. He will put it on a drip to stabilise the blood pressure.

Causes of shock:

- Cardiac arrest
- Severe bleeding
- Dehydration
- Bad fright
- Severe pain
- Poisoning
- Allergies
- Brain trauma
- Serious burns
- Severe stress
- Malignant tumours
- Septicaemia
- Sunstroke
- High fever
- Prolonged vomiting/ diarrhoea

Speedy actions can prevent the animal actually going into shock! If you see the following symptoms, you need to apply first aid immediately:

- Weak, irregular pulse
- Hectic, superficial breathing
- Cold ears and feet
- Pale skin (abdomen and inner thighs) and pale mucous membranes (mouth, eyes) and ears
- Apathy and anxiety

Epileptic seizure

A seizure can be very brief or rather long. The dog will fall over and stay lying in an abnormal position with convulsions. It may urinate, drool or have widened pupils.

After a seizure your dog will be exhausted and gasping from the exertion. The animal is dull and uncoordinated. An epileptic fit looks very serious and can cause panic in anyone witnessing it. With properly applied first aid, the whole situation is a lot less serious than it looks, therefore stay calm and proceed as follows:

- Carefully drag the dog by its back legs or body to a place where it cannot injure itself through its thrashing movements. For example, never leave it lying at the top of the stairs.
- Try to lessen the convulsions somewhat by putting a blanket or cloth over the animal and by surrounding it with cushions.

This also decreases the risk of the animal injuring itself.
- Never try to apply a halter or hold the animal in a restraining grip. Also don't give your dog any food, water or medication. (valium/diazepam suppositories)
- If necessary, apply mouth-to-mouth resuscitation. Watch your fingers when the dog starts breathing on its own again.
- Let the dog come round in a calm, dark environment. Stay and observe it for at least half an hour.
- If the seizures come back within short intervals, you are facing an emergency situation. Take the animal to the veterinarian as soon as possible.

Sunstroke
A dog may also be affected by heat. This often happens when the animal is left in a car for a long time, which is badly ventilated and standing in the sun. Sunstroke (or heatstroke) can be recognised by the following symptoms: fast, jerky breathing, a glazed look and a body temperature of more than 40ºC.

Take the animal to a shady, cool place. Immerse it in a bucket or tub of cold water or hose it down. Especially sparsely haired parts of the body, such as the belly, the elbows and the groin, need to be cooled off quickly. Stop with this when the body temperature drops below 39ºC. When the animal comes to, you need to dry it off and let it drink small amounts of water in intervals of a few minutes. Take the victim to the veterinarian as soon as possible.

5. Poisoning
If an animal has been poisoned, a number of different symptoms might appear. It will often have breathing problems, it will feel cold to touch and it might lose

consciousness. However, it might also be shaking and hyperactive. Always bear in mind that there is an increased chance of the animal going into shock.

Take the poison away from the dog as quickly as possible, but make sure that it doesn't become scared. Under no circumstances must the dog be frightened and run away. Remove any remnants of the poison from its mouth or the skin with a cloth as quickly as possible. Try to find out what the poison is. Take the package or whatever is left of the toxin to the veterinarian. This might be vital when it comes to determining the right antidote. How your dog has to be treated further depends on the type of poison it has ingested.

If your dog has ingested something from the group of non-caustic substances (see table), you need to make it vomit as quickly as possible. You can stimulate vomiting by placing a teaspoon of salt on the back of its tongue. Pick up some of the sick with a plastic bag and take it to the veterinarian. If the dog is unconscious, lay its head lower than the rest of the body. This allows the vomit to flow out of its mouth and prevents it from flowing into the lungs. If necessary, apply mouth-to-mouth resuscitation. If the animal cannot be taken to a vet immediately, it is best to wrap it in a blanket and to take it to a dark, quiet place. Sometimes you can read on packages of toxins which substances need to be administered as antidotes. If the dog has thrown up properly, you can give it a mix of milk and Norit. This is advisable if it will take some time before you can take your dog to the veterinarian.

If your pet has ingested a caustic substance (see table), it must not throw up under any circumstances! The mucous membranes of the mouth, throat and gullet have already been seriously damaged by the caustic toxin. If the toxin passes through them again, the damage will be more serious. Try to dilute the toxins in the digestive tract. In the case of a base toxin, give your dog vinegar or lemon juice. If your dog has ingested an acid, feed it soda or milk.

Non-caustic substances:	Caustic substances:
• Anti-freeze	• Base
• Bleach (chlorine)	- Caustic soda
• Carbamates	- Many paint or wallpaper strippers
• Pesticides:	• Petrol
- Strychnine	• Petroleum
- Crimidine	• Paint thinner
• Lead (paint and roof covering)	• Acids
• Insecticides:	- Battery acid
- Parathion	- Hydrochloric acid
- Dichlorvos	
• Snail poison	

6. Fractures
Broken bones
Unfortunately, dogs quite regularly have broken bones or fractures. The prominent cause of fractures is road traffic accidents, but a fall from great height, a bite by another animal or a gun shot wound may also lead to fractures. When applying first aid to fractures you need to be very careful, as the hard, sharp edges of the broken bone can easily damage tissues and organs.

We differentiate two types of fractures. In closed fractures the skin has not been damaged and the fractured parts are therefore not exposed to the air. In open fractures the fractured parts break out of the skin through the wound. This type of fracture can have serious consequences, as the very sensitive bone marrow can become infected by bacteria. Such an infection can make an animal seriously ill and will slow down the healing process of the fracture.

An open fracture is obviously easy to diagnose. In the case of a closed fracture this is a little more difficult. There are, however, some symptoms which indicate a fracture: pain, swelling, loss of function in the broken limb, abnormal position of the bone, abnormal mobility of the broken limb and a grating sound during movement. When you have clearly diagnosed a fracture, you should proceed as follows:
• Hold your dog in a restraining grip and let it calm down as much as possible at the scene of the accident.
• Be aware of shock symptoms. They may occur if your dog is in a lot of pain.
• Make sure that the broken leg lies on top.
• Do not pull on the leg and make sure that the fracture is as still as possible.
• If the lower part of the leg is broken and if you need to transport the animal quite a distance, apply a preliminary splint. This can be a straight piece of wood, a piece of carton or a rolled-up newspaper. Carefully apply cotton wool

or a thick cloth around the leg. Then apply the splints at the sides of the leg, so that the joints above and under the fracture can no longer move.
- Fasten the splints with tape or bandages, but don't pull them too tight. It is only a matter of immobilising the fracture for the time of transport, so that it doesn't move.
- Carefully push a blanket or board under the dog and lift the animal up. Make sure that it lies as quietly as possible.
- Take the animal to the veterinarian straight away.

In the case of an open fracture you need to make sure that the animal does not lick or scratch at the fracture. Put plenty of sterile gauze or a clean cloth onto the wound, so that no dirt can get into it. Do not put any salve or iodine onto it, as this only increases the risk of infection. The vet will need to treat an open fracture further.

7. Digestive tract
Vomiting
It is quite normal that dogs sometimes eat grass and throw up. They do this when their stomach bothers them. Eating grass stimulates vomiting, which means that the dog discards its stomach contents.

If a dog throws up too often, something is definitely wrong. Throwing up can have different causes, such as infections, worms, eating too much, poisoning and metabolism disturbances. Take your dog to the veterinarian as quickly as possible if it is throwing up heavily, throwing up blood and if it has a swollen belly and a very ill appearance.

If your dog throws up regularly, but does not appear sick otherwise, you can try out whether the symptoms disappear if you feed it easily digestible food and make an appointment with your vet. You sometimes need to feed your dog before bedtime to prevent so-called bile vomiting in the morning. You can buy special, easily digestible food at your pet shop or veterinarian for such cases. Divide the food into several portions per day, for example every two to four hours. Then the stomach gets the ideal opportunity to digest the food. Also make sure that your dog has plenty of fresh drinking water available. When the throwing up has stopped completely, you can carefully switch back to normal feeding. Start by replacing ten percent of the diet food with normal food. The next day you replace twenty percent, and so forth until the diet is once again a hundred percent normal food. If the problems haven't disappeared, you need to contact a vet.

Diarrhoea

When your dog's faeces are soft or watery, it is suffering from diarrhoea. This is a symptom of a disturbed digestion. This can have several causes, such as infection, worms, eating bad or cold food or a sudden change in the diet. If the diarrhoea is bloody, or if it is combined with symptoms such as fever, vomiting and apathy, take your dog to the veterinarian as soon as possible.

If your dog is suffering from light diarrhoea without being ill in any other way, feed it an easily digestible diet to solve the problem. Your vet or pet shop will have special, easily digestible feeds. Divide the feed into several smaller portions per day and feed it until the symptoms disappear, then slowly go back to normal food. This is best done by replacing ten percent of the diet food by normal food on the first day. On the second day you replace twenty percent and so on until the dog's diet consists of only normal food again. Always contact your vet if the diarrhoea doesn't stop; don't wait too long!

8. Other injuries
Bruises

To control the swelling, you can cover a bruise with a towel soaked in cold water or with ice cubes wrapped in a towel.

Traffic Accident Trauma

If you see a dog being hit by a car, don't run to it heedlessly. The last thing anyone needs in such a situation is another traffic victim! Immediately contact a vet or pet ambulance. Make sure that other drivers become aware of the victim by clearly marking the scene of the accident. If necessary, hold the victim in a restraining grip, carefully check if there are any bleeding wounds and treat the victim for shock. Carefully cover the dog with a coat or blanket. Let it lay quietly until professional help arrives. It is very important that you do not move the victim, even if no blood and wounds are visible at first sight, as the dog may have suffered internal injuries. You must also therefore not give the dog anything to drink until it has been examined by a vet.

Footpad injury
If your dog is walking awkwardly or licking its paw, there might be a splinter or another object stuck in the sole of its foot. You can carefully remove this with tweezers. Disinfect the spot with iodine straight away and bandage it. This prevents the dog licking at the wound and thus infecting it. In the case of heavy blood loss, or if the object is stuck deep in the sole, you need to take your dog to the veterinarian.

Choking
Dogs like to play with all sorts of things. It can therefore happen that the animal swallows something by accident. These can be a number of different objects, with different consequences ranging from serious to less acute. In the worst case, the swallowed object is stuck just before the windpipe. The animal can no longer breathe and this is obviously a life-threatening situation. An object which ends up in the gullet causes discomfort and sometimes a lot of pain, but the dog won't die of it immediately. You can recognise that an object is stuck in the gullet by the dog swallowing frequently and trying to throw up. The dog will drool a lot and rub its snout. In this case, proceed as follows:
- Hold your dog in a restraining grip if it doesn't want to accept your help.
- The dog will usually vomit; giving it food or water will only make things worse.
- An object in the gullet is a nuisance, but not life-threatening. Therefore remain calm. If the object is close to the windpipe, the animal will be in danger, which means that you need to act quickly.
- Open its mouth as far as possible and

look into its throat. If the sharp teeth make it difficult to hold the snout open, take a dry tissue to carefully pull out the tongue. The dog will keep its snout open, as it will not risk biting its tongue.

- If the object is clearly visible, you can carefully remove it with tweezers or small pliers. If an object is located just before the windpipe, you can sometimes remove it by putting a finger behind it, deep in the throat. Someone else will have to push on the right spot of the throat from the outside.
- If you don't succeed, lay the dog on its side on a hard surface.
- Apply pressure just behind the last ribs, where the thorax is widest. Push downwards and forwards with both hands. This sometimes makes the object shoot out of the throat.
- Repeat this action several times quickly after another if you don't succeed the first time. If the object is still stuck in the throat, try removing the object from the throat with your fingers, while someone else continues pressing behind the ribs.
- If necessary, apply mouth-to-mouth resuscitation.
- If the object has not been removed within a few minutes, take your dog to the veterinarian as quickly as possible. Even if you did manage to remove the object, your vet will still need to examine your dog for possible complications, such as damage to the throat or gullet. Do not take any risks opening the dog's mouth or removing an object, watch your hands and fingers!

Your dog may have swallowed a sharp object, such as a splinter or a fish bone. They will usually get caught in the mucous membranes of the mouth. In this case your dog will rub its snout a lot with its paw. It will also salivate excessively, sometimes mixed with blood, or retch. Some dogs might sit quietly in one corner, whereas others will run around the house like maniacs.

- Try to have a good look into your dog's throat. If necessary, apply a restraining grip.
- If you localised the sharp object, you can carefully try to remove it. If it is stuck very tightly, leave it in the mouth.
- Carefully wipe the froth from the oral cavity and take your dog to the veterinarian as quickly as possible.
- During your journey, hold onto your dog's paws, so that it cannot injure itself by continuously rubbing against its snout.
- Your vet will remove the object, probably under anaesthetic. After this, your dog will have some problems eating and will need to be fed an adjusted diet.

Wounds

A dog can become wounded in a number of ways. You may therefore encounter a wide range of wounds, which vary in their severity. Roughly, you can divide them into simple wounds, in which only the skin surface has been damaged and complex wounds, in which deeper layers, such as muscles, blood vessels and nerves have also been affected. Both types obviously need to be treated in their own way.

Always take your dog to the veterinarian if it has suffered a severe wound. Graze wounds are best cleaned with warm boiled water.

More danger

Our modern houses actually are a very strange environment for animals. There are no trees, no grass, and no shrubs. The wind does not blow around their ears. There is no stream with fresh water and no trees to scratch on. An animal needs to adapt. This does not always go smoothly, but we can make sure that its life with us is as safe as possible.

Plants

It is common knowledge that cats sometimes like to eat grass. Dogs do this too. You never know what a dog sees in a plant. Puppies in particular occasionally like to take a bite. The likelihood isn't big, but if it does happen, take your dog and a branch of the plant in question to your vet. He will know the best course of action.

We will provide a short overview of toxic plants.

TOXIC PLANTS

-A-

Abrus precatorius	- Precatory-pea
Acer rubrum	- Red maple
Aconitum napellus	- Monk's hood
Aesculus hippocastanum	- Horse chestnut
Ailanthus altissima	- Tree-of-heaven
Allamanda cathartica	- Golden-trumper
Allium cepa	- Onion
Allium sativum	- Garlic
Alstroemeria ligtu	- Peruvian lily
Amaranthus hybridus	- Smooth pigweed
Amaryllis vittata	- Amaryllis (*A. vittata*)
Anthurium andraenum	- Flamingo lily
Aquilegia alpina	- Aquilegia
Asimina triloba	- Pawpaw

Aquilegia

-B-

Baptista tinctoria	- Wild indigo
Barbarea vulgaris	- Yellow rocket
Buxus sempervirens	- Buxus

Buxus

-C-

Caladium bicolor	- Caladium
Chrysanthemum indicum	- Chrysanthemum
Cicuta virosa	- Northern water-hemlock
Clematis	- Clematis
Clivia miniata	- Kaffir lily
Codiaeum variegetum	- Croton
Colchicum autumnale	- Autumn crocus
Conium macaltum	- Poison-hemlock
Convallaria majalis	- Lily-of-the-valley
Corydalis	- Corydalis
Crocus	- Crocus
Cyclamen persicum	- Cyclamen

Clematis

-D-

Dature innoxia	- Angel's trumpet
Datura stramonium	- Jimsomweed
Delphinium	- Larkspur
Dieffenbachia seguine	- Mother-in-law-plant
Digitalis purpurea	- Foxglove

Corydalis

-E-

Euonymus europaeus	- European spindletree
Euphorbia helioscopia	- Sun spurge
Euphorbia lacteal	- Candelabra-cactus
Euphorbia pulcherrima	- Poinsettia

Crocus

-F-

Fagopyrum esculentem	- Tall manna grass

-G-

Gutierrezia sarothrae	- Broom snakewood
Gymnocladus dioicus	- Kentucky coffeetree

-H-

Hedera helix	- English ivy
Helenium autumnale	- Sneezeweed
Helianthus annuus	- Sunflower
Heliotropium curassavicum	- Spatulate-leaved heliotrope
Heracleum mantegazzianum	- Giant hogweed
Humulus lupulus	- Common hop
Hyancinthoides nonscripta	- English bluebell
Hydrangea macrophylla	- Hydrangea
Hypercum perforatum	- St. John's wort

-I-

Ilex aquifolium	- English holly
Ipomoea tricolour	- Morning glory
Iris pseudocorus	- Yellow iris
Iris versicolor	- Blue flag iris

-J-

Juglans nigra	- Black walnut

-K-

Kalanchoe daigremontiana	- Devil's-backbone
Kalmia angustofolia	- Sheep-laurel

-L-

Laportea canadensus	- Canada nettle
Lathyrus odoratus	- Sweet pea
Lathyrus sativus	- Grass pea
Leonurus cardiaca	- Motherwort
Ligistrum vulgare	- Common privet
Linaria vulgaris	- Yellow toadflax
Lobelia cardinalis	- Cardinalflower
Lobelia inflate	- Indian-tobacco
Lonicera xylosteum	- Fly honeysuckle
Lupinus argenteus	- Silvery lupine
Lupinus polyphyllus	- Large-leaved lupine
Lupinus pusillus	- Small lupine
Lupinus sericeus	- Silky lupine

-M-

Mangifera indica	- Mango
Medicago sativa	- Alfalfa
Melilotus alba	- White sweet clover
Melitus officinalis	- Yellow sweet clover
Menispermum canadense	- Moonseed
Monstera deliciosa	- Swiss-cheese plant

-N-

Narcissus peoticus	- Narcissus
Narcissus pseudonarcissus	- Daffodil

Delphinium

Datura   Digitalis

Euonymus

Hedera   Hydrangea

Ilex   Lonicera

| Nerium oleander | - Oleander |
| Nicotiana tabacum | - Tobacco |

-O-

Onoclea sensibilis	- Sensitive fern
Ornithogalum umbellatum	- Star-of-Bethlehem
Oxytropus lambertii	- Purple locoweed

-P-

Lupinus

Papaver nudicaule	- Iceland poppy
Papaver orientale	- Oriental poppy
Papaver somniferum	- Opium poppy
Parthenocissus quinquefolia	- Virginia creeper
Persea americana	- Avocado
Phacelia campanularia	- California canarygrass
Phalaris arundinacea	- Reed canarygrass
Philodendron cordatum	- Philodendron
Phoradendron flavescens	- American mistletoe
Physalis alkekengi	- Chinese-lantern
Physalis peruviana	- Ground-cherry
Phytolacca american	- Pokeweed
Pinus ponderosa	- Ponderosa pine
Primula obconica	- Primula
Polygonatum multiflorum	- Solomon's seal
Prunus pennsylvanica	- Pin cherry
Ptedidium aquilinum	- Bracken

Papaver orientalis

-Q-

| Quercus alba | - White oak |
| Quercus rubra | - Red oak |

-R-

Parthenocissus

Rananculus bulbosus	- Bulbous buttercup
Raphanus raphanistrum	- Wild radish
Raphanus sativus	- Radish
Rhamnus carthartica	- European buckthorn
Rheum rhaponticum	- Rhubarb
Rhododendron macrophyllum	- California rose-baby
Rhus diversiloba	- Western poison-oak
Rhus radicans	- Poison ivy
Ricinus communis	- Castor-bean
Robinia pseudoacacia	- Black locust
Rudbeckia serotina	- Black-eyed Susan
Rumex acetosa	- Garden sorrel

Phytolacca

-S-

Sambucus canadensis	- American elder
Sambucus nigra	- European elder
Sarcobatus vermiculatus	- Greasewood
Scilla siberica	- Siberian scilla
Senecop jacobaea	- Tansy ragwort
Sinapis arvensis	- Wild mustard
Solanum dulcamara	- Climbing nightshade
Solanum nigrum	- Black nightshade
Solanum speudocapsicum	- Jerusalem-cherry

Polygonatum   Rhododendron

Solanum tuberosum	- Potato
Solidago mollis	- Velvety goldenrod
Sorghum halepense	- Johnson grass
Suckleya suckleyana	- Poison suckleya
Symphoricarpos albus	- Thin-leaved snowberry
Symphytum asperum	- Prickly comfrey
Symplocarpus foetidus	- Skunk cabbage

-T-

Tanacetum vulgare	- Tansy
Taxus canadensis	- Canada yew
Thermopsis rhombifolia	- Golden-bean
Thlaspi arvense	- Stinkweed
Thuja	- Thuja
Trifolium pratense	- Red clover
Trifolium repens	- White clover
Tulipa gesneriana	- Tulip

-U-

Urica dioica	- Stinging nettle

-V-

Veratrum viride	- False hellebore
Viburnum opulus	- Guelder-rose
Vicia sativa	- Common vetch

-W-

Wisteria floribunda	- Japanese wisteria

-X-

Xanthium strumarium	- Cocklebur

-Z-

Zigadenus elegans	- White camas

Ricinus

Sedum spectabile

Thuja

Other dangers

A human walks on two legs and doesn't always see what can happen at ankle and knee height. You could say that anything that may be dangerous for a crawling baby can also be dangerous for a dog. We will give you a few examples.

Cables

Young dogs like to bite into all sorts of things like wires from lamps, the computer and other electric appliances. These can be found everywhere in the house. Hide these as far as possible. You can also buy certain materials to wrap around cables and thus protect them.

Detergents

Although most people don't think of detergents as being immediate hazards for dogs, they contain substances which are toxic for dogs.

So it is self-explanatory that you should not let your dog walk over them or spray it with detergents, but danger is still lurking around the corner. Just take simple mopping of the floor, something you will have to do more regularly if you have pets.

Whichever cleaning equipment you use, at a certain point the floor is wet while you are working. If the dog walks over the wet floor, it will also get detergent on its paws. If the dog licks its paws dry again it will then ingest toxic detergent.

Chocolate

Sometimes we think that what we see on television is actually true. In cartoons, but also in some programmes, there is a strange notion of dogs and sweets. Don't be tempted to think that what dogs eat in cartoons is actually the right food for dogs in real life. Chocolate is one of those products that humans enjoy, but which is actually toxic for dogs and cats. Chocolate contains certain substances which their bodies cannot break down. So never feed a dog chocolate and definitely don't let it scavenge around. Luckily, most cats don't like sweet foods, but dogs do!

Tips

- Select and buy a puppy via the breed association.
- Try to visit several breeders before buying a puppy.
- The first car trip is quite an experience for your puppy. Plan this trip as part of your training and make it an educational and pleasant experience.
- Yorkies and Silkies are lively dogs, but they cannot stand a hard hand.
- Yorkies and Silkies can be quite stubborn, so be consistent in their upbringing.
- Never leave you little dog unattended on a chair or table. It can hurt itself when trying to jump off.
- Attend a puppy course with your dog. It's is fun for two and you'll both learn a lot.
- Ignore timid or submissive behaviour and don't be tempted to comfort your dog.
- Give plenty of attention to your dog's silky coat every day.
- Don't fight just fleas, but also fight flea larvae.
- Specially formulated diet and chews help to on keep a dog's teeth healthy.
- Never buy a puppy if you have not been able to see its mother.
- Make sure your dog doesn't get too fat or heavy. It is very bad for its health. Not too much to eat and plenty of exercise is the golden rule.

Internet

A great deal of information can be found on the internet. A selection of websites with interesting details and links to other sites and pages is listed here. Sometimes pages move to another site or address. You can find more sites by using the available search-engines.

For Great Britain

www.the-kennel-club.org.uk
The Kennel Club's primary objective is to promote, in every way, the general improvement of dogs. This site aims to provide you with information you may need to be a responsible pet owner and to help you keep your dog happy, safe and content.

http://en.wikipedia.org/ wiki/Yorkshire_Terrier
A lot of information about appearance, coat and colour, built and proportions, modification, temperament, health, hypoglycaemia and lots more.

http://en.wikipedia.org/ wiki/Australian_Silky_Terrier
Information about appearance, temperament and history and links.

www.k9-care.co.uk
The Self-Help site for dog owners. A beautiful website with tons of information on dogs. All you need to know about grooming, training, health care, buying a dog, travel and much more.

www.pethealthcare.co.uk
At PEThealthcare.co.uk they believe that a healthy pet is a happy pet. Which is why they've brought together leading experts to create a comprehensive online source of pet care information.

For U.S.A.

www.ytca.org
Yorkshire Terrier Club of America, Inc. All about the breed, breed standard, Club info, history, FAQ, grooming, sports, shows and show kalender.

www.aboutpets.info
The website of the publisher of the About Pets book series. An overview of the titles, availability in which languages and where in the world the books are sold.

Addresses

Becoming a member of a breed club or association can be very useful for good advice and interesting activities. Contact The Kennel Club in case addresses or telephone numbers have changed.

Being a member of a breed association gives you background information about your dog. You receive a club magazine. Club members come together for meetings and lectures organised by your club.

When becoming a member you are always up to date about developments of your breed.

After all, who would miss an evening about grooming a Yorkshire terrier or Australian Silky terrier? Feel free to contact any of these associations:

For Great Britain

**Cheshire & North Wales
Yorkshire Terrier Society**
Secretary: Mrs J Milner
Tel No: 0151 3272276

Midland Yorkshire Terrier Club
Secretary: Mrs K Slaney
Tel No: 01283 226189

**Eastern Counties
Yorkshire Terrier Club**
Secretary: Mrs Pooley
For further information contact The Kennel Club

**Lincoln & Humberside
Yorkshire Terrier Club**
Secretary: Mrs B Pipes
Tel No: 01904 631961

**Northern Counties
Yorkshire Terrier Club**
Secretary: Ms Watson
Tel No: 01226 781373

**South Western
Yorkshire Terrier Club**
Secretary: Mrs J Drake
Tel No: 0117 9601592

Ulster Yorkshire Terrier Club
Secretary: Mr S. Larkham
Tel No: 02893 378302

**Yorkshire Terrier
Club of South Wales**
Secretary: Mr T M Evans
Tel No: 01443 431052

Yorkshire Terrier Club
Secretary: Mrs P E Mitchell
Tel No: 01235 833171

Yorkshire Terrier Club of Scotland
Secretary: Ms Burns
Tel No: 01592 759277

Australian Silky Terrier Society
Secretary: Miss A Marshall
Tel No: 01253 868175

For U.S.A.

American Kennel Club
The AKC provides coverage on all accepted breeds. Gives information on registration, pedigrees and dog shows. Look at the website! So much to see about breeders, breeds, registration, addresses and events.
www.akc.org

United Kennel Club
The United Kennel Club was established in 1898. It is the largest all-breed performance-dog registry in the world, registering dogs from all 50 states and 25 foreign countries.
UKC
100 E Kilgore Rd Kalamazoo MI
49002 - 5584
Office hours: 9:00 to 4:30 p.m.
(E.S.T.) Monday through Friday.
Phone: 269 - 343 - 9020
Fax: 269 - 343 - 7037

Breed association

**Yorkshire Terrier Club
of America, Inc.**
Secretary : Shirley Patterson
Address: 2102 Chestnut Ct
Pottstown
PA , 19465-7163
Email: sptoydogs@aol.com

Profile

The Yorkshire terrier
Group: Toy
Country of origin: Great Britain
Original task: Pest control
Present task: Companion and show dog
Character: Lively, loyal, inquisitive, obedient
Colour: Steel-blue with tan
Particular needs: Intensive daily coat care
Height: Approximately 23 cm
Weight: 2.5 tot 3.5 kg
Life expectancy: 12 to 15 years

Australian Silky terrier
Group: Toy
Country of origin: Australia
Original task: Companion and show dog
Character: Assertive, lively, affectionate and clever
Colour: Blue and tan or grey-blue and tan
Particular needs: Intensive daily coat care
Height: Approximately 23 cm,
Bitches a little smaller
Weight: 3.5 to 4.5 kg
Life expectancy: 12 to 15 years